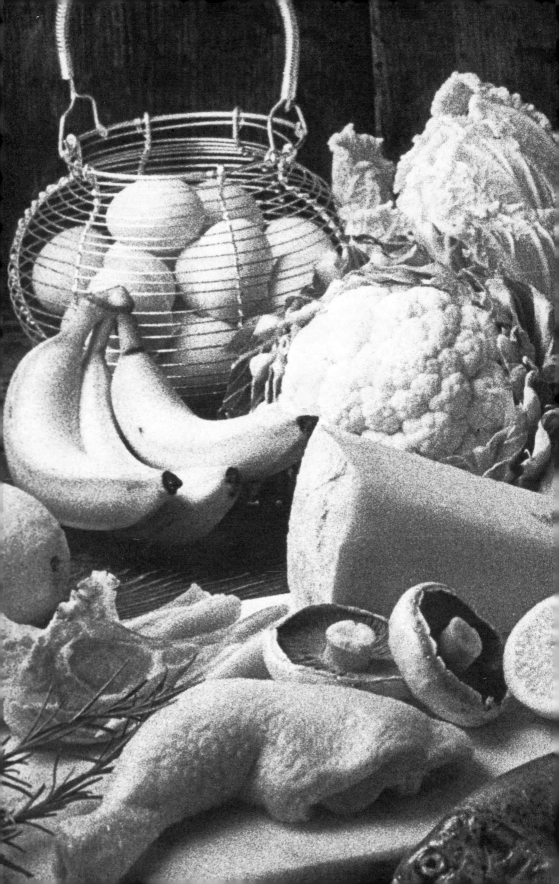

Delia Smith's
One is fun!

HODDER AND STOUGHTON
LONDON SYDNEY AUCKLAND TORONTO

The publishers would like to thank the following for the loan of equipment and accessories for the photographs: Harrods, Liberty's, The Conran Shop, David Mellor and Divertimenti for china and cutlery; Descamps for tablecloths and napkins and Osborne and Little for material.

Design: Roger Judd

British Library Cataloguing in Publication Data
Smith, Delia
   Delia Smith's one is fun!
   1. Cookery
   I. Title
   641.5'.61   TX652
   ISBN 0-340-37377-6

First published in Great Britain 1985. Eleventh impression 1994.

Published by Hodder and Stoughton,
a division of Hodder Headline PLC,
338 Euston Road, London NW1 3BH

Photoset by Rowland Phototypesetting Limited, Bury St Edmunds, Suffolk.

Printed and bound in Great Britain by
Butler & Tanner Ltd, Frome and London

List of Colour Plates

Photographs by Barry Bullough
Home economist: Anne Page-Wood

By the same author

Frugal Food
How to Cheat at Cooking
Evening Standard Cook Book
Delia Smith's Book of Cakes
Delia Smith's Complete Cookery Course

For M. I.

As always a very special thank you to Michael, my husband, without whose help this book would not have been possible. Special thanks to Mary Cox for her invaluable help in testing all the recipes.

Contents

Conversion tables

All these are *approximate* conversions, which have either been rounded up or down. In a few recipes it has been necessary to modify them very slightly. Never mix metric and imperial measures in one recipe, stick to one system or the other. All spoon measurements used throughout this book are level unless specified otherwise.

Oven temperatures

Mark 1	275°F	140°C
2	300	150
3	325	170
4	350	180
5	375	190
6	400	200
7	425	220
8	450	230
9	475	240

Volume

1 fl oz	25 ml
2	55
2½	60
3	75
5 (¼ pt)	150
½ pt	275
12	330
¾ pt	425
1	570
1¾	1 litre

Weights

½ oz	10 g
¾	20
1	25
1½	40
2	50
2½	60
3	75
4	110
4½	125
5	150
6	175
7	200
8	225
9	250
10	275
12	350
1 lb	450
1½	700
2	900
3	1 kg 350 g

Measurements

⅛ inch	3 mm
¼	5 mm
½	1 cm
¾	2
1	2·5
1¼	3
1½	4
1¾	4·5
2	5
3	7·5
4	10
5	13
6	15
7	18
8	20
9	23
10	25·5
11	28
12	30

Introduction

I once worked for an editor who described a typical meal in his bachelor days as sitting alone in front of the television with an open jar of commercially made tartare sauce into which he dunked his fish fingers before consuming them. Perhaps it was he who first planted the seeds of concern in me that eventually motivated me to write this book. But apart from him there have been scores of requests and pleas from people – not just from those who live alone but also from others who, for one reason or another, find themselves having to serve single-portion meals.

The complaint I receive most frequently is that all recipes are family-oriented, and that it *is* extremely difficult to scale down ingredients, utensils and timings. Just before writing this introduction I was stopped by a man in a supermarket. 'Can you help me?' he asked. 'I love your pâté, but I live alone and the recipe makes 3½ lb!' I was delighted to explain to him that at last I had taken heed of the plight of lone cooks and was writing this book exclusively for them.

First, though, I must clarify a couple of points that relate to cooking for one. Most important, I would like to stress that this is precisely what the book is about: *cooking* for one. If, like my former editor, you are the kind of person who hates to cook, who gets satisfaction from pouring boiling water over instant gravy granules, then I'm afraid this book is not for you. I am very aware that there are people who are simply not interested in what they eat and I have written for them elsewhere; but neither do I share the dismissive opinion of the lady who commented: 'People on their own? All they want is a yoghurt.' How strange that people on their own (who actually outnumber the family groups in this country) should be victims of culinary discrimination.

I think we accept too readily that eating is a social occasion, therefore if you are on your own you are already failing to fulfil one of the important criteria for a proper meal. One of the subtlest but, I suspect, most pervasive problems in modern society is that (often carefully hidden) lack of self-acceptance, and I really believe that a conscious effort to care for ourselves – especially when eating, which we do two or three times a day – is a most marvellous antidote to this. Eating (and cooking) an interesting, satisfying meal does make, I am certain, a great contribution to our feeling of well-being.

I began this book wanting to help people to overcome the practical difficulties, but ended up discovering there were equally important psychological difficulties. 'It hardly seems worth the bother just for me.' It *is* worth the bother, but until you've bothered you won't discover the satisfaction. It isn't easy to break out of the instant convenience-living syndrome, but it can be done by stages. For instance, instead of downing your thin, half-cold cup of dreaded instant coffee – cold because it's too boring to gain your attention – buy yourself a small cafetière and sit down to really enjoy sipping and *savouring* a cup of freshly ground coffee. It works wonders psychologically.

What I myself have discovered, to my joy, is that cooking for one *really is fun*. Unlike cooking for a family, the labour and amount of equipment needed are minimal and the recipes, for the most part, are quicker. If you are prepared to invest a little time shopping for the right ingredients, I promise you that good food for one is not just a possibility, it's a guarantee, every night of the week.

Finally, I ought to add that all the recipes in this book are easily multiplied by two, three or even four. So if you are expecting company – or are cooking for a family – you won't have to look elsewhere.

Shopping

Shopping for one used to be far more difficult than it is today. At long last most supermarkets offer smaller prepacked portions of meat and fish, and the new trend towards self-selection (that is, picking out however much you need of an item and paying by weight) is a godsend to those who only want small amounts. Of course it is even better to buy your requirements from the butcher, fishmonger or greengrocer: in that case you don't have to put up with taking an ounce more or less than you need (as is the case with prepackaged items). The only barrier here is the psychological one. Some people tell me it is a little embarrassing asking for very small quantities. Don't let it be. After all people who have to cook just for themselves represent some twenty per cent of the whole country – the shopkeepers couldn't afford to lose all that custom! And don't be afraid to ask the butcher or fishmonger to do the jobs he is skilled at – and are so difficult to do at home, like filleting and boning.

Planning: if you're just cooking for yourself and can only shop once a week, then it does help to plan ahead. I say this as one of the world's worst planners, but cooking and shopping for the recipes in this book have made me realise the value of planning. For instance, if you have decided on a recipe that calls for half an aubergine, then why not consider another recipe that also calls for half an aubergine, shop for that as well and have it later in the week?

Mixed Doubles: because you can save a great deal of time by cooking certain things in double quantity (to make two meals), I have indicated some recipes that can be prepared in tandem as it were – and these I have called 'Mixed Doubles'. The whole concept, however, can only work to your advantage if you remember to shop for both recipes at the same time.

Fresh produce: the dilemma we have to confront here is, on the one hand, what is the ideal and, on the other hand, how much of that ideal can be reconciled with reality? Ideally, we should shop every day to ensure absolute freshness; in reality, this is simply not possible for most people.

You cannot, for example, buy a quarter of a green pepper yet that is what is called for in some of the recipes here. So for one person storing is inevitable. I have found throughout this book that it is quite possible to store most fresh vegetables in the fridge, in tied polythene bags with a few holes punched in them, for up to five days. Obviously all fruit and vegetables need to be purchased in peak condition: if they're bruised or shrivelled to start with they won't even keep for a day.

Equipment

The first problem I had to face when I began this book was how to get round the economic absurdity of heating up a large amount of oven space to cook a single portion, without confining everything to the grill or frying-pan. Microwave was not the answer because it is still only an 'also-ran' item of equipment and cannot in any event entirely replace the combination of oven, hob and grill (and I doubted whether many people on their own would be the owners of two ovens!).

Ovens

The ideal oven for one – if you are contemplating buying one – is the double oven, which comprises a smaller oven for everyday cooking, and a larger one which could be used when entertaining. However there is an excellent alternative for the person living alone, and this is the table-top oven. Some of these have no grill or hob, but one of them, the British-made Baby Belling, has both, as well as a good-sized oven. It is portable and works off an ordinary 13-amp plug. It would be my choice for anyone who doesn't wish to invest in a full-sized cooker.

Hobs and grills

One of the challenges of trying to avoid using costly oven space was in testing out the full potential and versatility of the hob and grill. In fact a surprising number of dishes can be cooked under the grill, in foil or otherwise, as you will discover from the recipes later in the book. The crucial part of this exercise is getting the food the correct distance from the heat, so it is worth checking before you start that your grill pan or rack can be set the required distance from the grill.

The recurring problem with cooking small amounts on top of the stove is simmering. The last thing you want is the frustration of not being able to get your liquid down to the *gentle* simmer that is essential for long cooking (in my kitchen my ceramic hob may be utterly incapable of bringing 6 lb of marmalade to a rolling boil, but it does come into its own when gentle simmering is called for). A gentle simmer I would define as a few small bubbles steadily breaking through the surface of the liquid you are cooking. If this is not possible with your hob, then I suggest you invest in a metal heat-diffuser: place this over the flame or radiant ring when you want to simmer gently, place the saucepan or casserole on top of that, and all should be well.

Pots and pans

I have written extensively elsewhere about the absolute necessity of using the right equipment for cooking. I don't pretend that it can all be obtained at once, but someone who cares about food will take the trouble to build up a stock of essential equipment gradually. And the one thing that my twenty-two years of cookery has taught me (to my cost) is that good, solid equipment – though initially more expensive – works out far cheaper in the long run.

All the recipes in this book can actually be followed with a minimum amount of equipment, as I have taken care to use more or less the same size for everything. If you intend to do a lot of cooking for one, then the items below are the perfect choice:

One 5½ inch (14 cm) cast-iron enamelled saucepan
One 7 inch (18 cm) medium cast-iron enamelled saucepan
One 7 inch (18 cm) round flameproof cast-iron enamelled casserole
One heavy-based 7 inch (18 cm) (base measurement) frying-pan
One 9 inch (23 cm) oval flameproof cast-iron enamelled gratin dish
One round French flameproof gratin dish (6 inch (15 cm) base measurement)
Three ovenproof soufflé or ramekin dishes – one 3 inch (7·5 cm) base measurement, one 4 inch (10 cm) base measurement, and the other 5 inch (13 cm) base measurement

I have come to the conclusion that the very best make of saucepan, casserole and frying-pan for one on offer at present is Le Creuset. They are in the top price bracket but are a sound investment. Recently they have also brought out a non-stick range called Castoflan, which includes a lipped saucepan (called a milk pan) which is a joy to make sauces in and rinses clean in seconds.

Care of equipment

New pots and pans need to be seasoned before use, so always follow the manufacturer's instructions. Also, if you're using enamelled cast-ironware, remember not to over-heat it – for instance, after browning meat over a high heat, turn it down immediately.

Other items

Sharp knives are part of the general cooking equipment. The knives I recommend are Swiss-made by a firm called Victorinox. Some of these are illustrated on page 14, but there are also two not illustrated that I would like to recommend. One is a small serrated knife called a tomato knife which doesn't need sharpening and the other a small potato parer. The address for the stockists is on page 214. The recipes in this book do call for a pestle and mortar: although you can improvise with a pudding basin and the end of a rolling-pin, a pestle and mortar will make life very much easier. The other piece of equipment that comes into this category is some kind of blender, liquidiser or food processor (though, with the small quantities involved in this book, the latter is rather an indulgence). Any other essential equipment appears in the photo on page 14.

Ingredients

Storecupboard ingredients

The following is a list of straightforward ingredients that crop up, more than once, in the recipes that follow. Shopping will be so much easier if you can keep a stock of these always to hand: capers, gherkins, Worcestershire sauce, mushroom ketchup, tomato purée, anchovies, tuna fish, olives, preserved green peppercorns, mustard powder, walnuts, preserved stem ginger, rock salt, whole black peppercorns, wine vinegar, olive oil, Tabasco sauce.

Tinned Italian chopped tomatoes

These deserve a special mention, as they are indispensable in the winter months when the imported fresh tomatoes are colourless and flavourless. I have found the Sainsbury's brand excellent both for flavour and texture. A heaped tablespoon of chopped tomatoes is the equivalent of one medium-sized peeled tomato, and you'll be glad to know that whatever is left over in the tin can be stored (in a glass or porcelain jug), covered with clingfilm, in the fridge for five days.

Spices

Below is a list of spices that are included in the recipes here. Ready-ground spices have such a short shelf-life that it makes them most uneconomical for one, so you would be well advised, wherever possible, to buy whole spices and grind them when required with pestle and mortar.

Whole cumin seeds	Whole coriander seeds
Whole cardamom pods	Crushed dried chilli/chilli powder
Whole nutmeg	Cinnamon sticks
Chinese star anise	Powdered turmeric
Juniper berries	Madras (or hot) curry powder

Cheese

Fresh grated Parmesan is a *must* for any cook. The ready-grated kind in packets is no substitute so far as flavour is concerned. Mozzarella crops up in these recipes several times. If you can get it (and don't have to store it for long) fresh Mozzarella is ideal; but it is also possible to buy Danish Mozzarella, which does keep well and is fine for cooking.

Herbs

In the summer months these are widely available from greengrocers and some supermarkets. But with the quantities involved in recipes for one, a single cook can do very well from herbs grown from seed in a windowbox, harvesting a few basil leaves, snipped chives or whatever as and when they are needed.

As for the winter, it is my firm belief that a supply of some dried herbs is better than none at all. Some people can get quite sniffy at the very mention of dried herbs, but the fact is that while some herbs do not dry very satisfactorily, many are more than passable (if not kept for too long). Among these I would include:

Dill	Tarragon	Basil	Bayleaves
Dried mixed herbs	Oregano	Rosemary	Thyme

Oriental ingredients

One thing we have to thank television for is that the various cookery programmes over the past decade have encouraged many people all over the country to ask for unusual, and hitherto unobtainable, ingredients. The shops in turn have responded to this demand, and the result is a much greater availability of Indian, Chinese and other ingredients.

Fresh root ginger: this I have used extensively in the book, as it has such a wonderfully pungent and fragrant aroma. Buy it in small quantities: it keeps well in a cool place, wrapped in clingfilm, for about a week. If you want to store it for longer, Elizabeth David in her book *Salts, Spices and Aromatics* recommends peeling it then storing it covered with sherry in a small screwtop jar. I have used this method and it works like a dream for several months. I keep mine in the fridge and just grate a little off as and when I need it.

Soy sauce: there are a number of synthetic imitations of this around, so it's worthwhile going to a healthfood store, delicatessen or Chinese shop for the genuine kind made from fermented soy bean. All the recipes in this book call for the dark soy sauce.

Dried mushrooms: you'll have no trouble locating these in Chinese stores, but they're also obtainable from many Italian shops and health-food stores. They come in several varieties and have a beautifully concentrated flavour. To use them, simply presoak them in warm water for thirty minutes. They may strike you as expensive, but you actually need very little since they swell up in the water. If you use a little dried mushroom along with some fresh in a recipe, you get a considerably enhanced mushroom flavour.

Chinese dried shrimps: these are magnificent, though alas are at present only available in Chinese shops. They have twice the flavour of frozen peeled prawns, they are much cheaper and you can store them almost indefinitely. Like the mushrooms they need to be soaked in warm water for thirty minutes before use.

Creamed coconut: this is a block (easily grated) of pure condensed coconut containing the essential coconut oil. It is used to flavour and thicken curries, in particular, and is stocked by most supermarkets.

Rice noodles: these are the nicest noodles of all. You don't have to cook them, just presoak them for ten minutes. They are available from Chinese shops (*see page 214*).

Booze for cooking

If you've taken the pledge, by all means abandon alcohol and substitute stock in savoury recipes, fruit juice in sweet recipes. Otherwise I go along with the bible which speaks of 'wine that cheers men's hearts'. It certainly cheers many a recipe, and whereas it would once have been unthinkable to open a bottle of wine merely to provide 2 fl oz for a recipe, wine now comes packaged in smaller and smaller bottles, not to mention ring-pull cans and boxes complete with taps.

I have therefore indulged quite a lot throughout this book, but wherever appropriate I have also suggested dry cider as a splendid – and more economical – alternative. But when all's said and done, there *is* something pretty cheerful about pouring a little wine into a recipe and the rest into a glass to go with it. Dry sherry is also a good friend to cooks, both for use in the recipes and to sip while you await the conclusion. It serves as a good substitute for rice wine in Chinese recipes.

Healthy eating

No book can get away without at least a mention of this topic nowadays, with the constant warnings of doctors and nutritionists on the effects of high-fat and low-fibre intakes ringing in our ears.

I think that, as a general rule, it is the responsibility of each one of us individually to assess our eating habits and take the appropriate action. Therefore I have not called for low-cholesterol margarine or added bran and so on in these recipes, largely because that would assume (rather impertinently, it seems to me) that everyone I am writing for *is* eating too much animal fat or not enough fibre.

What I always advocate is balance. Some of these recipes do indeed include butter (for sweating vegetables or making sauces for instance), but the amount is usually minimal and, unless you are already spreading butter on bread so thick your teeth leaves marks in it, it is not likely to be excessive (personally I spread my bread with a low-fat dairy spread like Gold and I find this gives me a little licence with butter for cooking). Also, wherever possible in these recipes, I have used groundnut or olive oil in preference to other fats.

However, if you *do* need to cut your cholesterol intake, then by all means use a low-cholesterol fat for cooking. The same applies to the cream used in some of the recipes – again the amount is minimal and since cream does lift so many sauces into a different class, I can find no reason to abandon it entirely. Yoghurt, or a mixture of half-cream and half-yoghurt, could be used instead. But as I said, I'm not prescribing anything: it has to be a personal decision.

Solo Soups

One is fun!

An old friend of mine recently recalled that her childhood in France had included a fresh soup every day. Her mother, she said, would make anything into a soup: she would even go off and gather young nettles if nothing else was to hand! I doubt whether nowadays a working mother – French or otherwise – would go to such lengths for a soup.

It's a sad fact that homemade soups have become a rarity. But I continue to hold the view that, while they may be particularly tempting for the solo cook, tinned or packet soups are bad news. Not just in the culinary sense, but psychologically as well. In spite of modern food technology their flavour today is as boring as it was a couple of decades ago. Clearly they are sold to people who have little interest in food or eating: for anyone who really cares about what he or she eats, a tinned soup can become more depressing with every spoonful.

The soups in this chapter are made for the most part from fresh ingredients, but what is more, they are all quick. And they have one other important thing in common: they have been devised not as an overture to a meal (which for one person would be something of an indulgence) but as the main part of the programme. I am suggesting, in other words, that these soups (followed perhaps by just fruit or cheese) should constitute a meal in themselves – which explains why the portions are generous and substantial. Those with smaller appetites could well decide to put some by as a starter for the next day.

A final word – about stock. We tend to forget nowadays that fresh ingredients have a lot of flavour of their own to impart. That flavour is sometimes delicate and can be overwhelmed by a strong stock or stock cubes (which almost invariably seem to me to introduce an incompatible taste). In most cases plain water is all that's needed; but if you find that difficult I have included a very quick vegetable stock recipe which will serve you well.

Ten-minute stock

Time and again I have tried to use stock cubes but have always come to the same conclusion – which is that they so often introduce an alien flavour into the recipe (even when you use less than the recommended amount).

I therefore prefer to use either plain water, or water enriched with a little tomato purée or mushroom ketchup – depending on the recipe. However, it is possible to make a light stock for soups for one, if you prefer that, and the following can be made in just ten minutes.

a 3-inch piece of celery (7·5 cm), cut in half lengthways
1 small carrot, split in half lengthways
1 small onion, sliced
a few parsley stalks and celery leaves
6 black peppercorns
1 bayleaf
a little salt
½–¾ pint cold water (275–425 ml)

Simply place all the ingredients in a small saucepan, cover with a lid, bring everything up to the boil, and boil briskly for 10 minutes. Then strain (and discard) the vegetables, and the stock is ready to use.

Smoked haddock chowder with poached egg

This really is a complete meal in itself – though if you're very hungry you might even like to put two eggs into it!

6 oz smoked haddock (175 g)
6 fl oz milk (175 ml)
6 fl oz water (175 ml)
1 bayleaf
½ oz butter (10 g)
½ smallish onion, finely chopped
1 level teaspoon flour
1 dessertspoon lemon juice
1 large egg
1 dessertspoon chopped parsley
salt and freshly milled black pepper

Begin by placing the haddock in a medium-sized saucepan, then pour in the milk and water and season with some freshly milled pepper (but no salt yet) and add a bayleaf. Gently bring the fish up to simmering point and simmer very gently for 5 minutes. Then take it off the heat, pour it all into a bowl and leave it to steep for about 15 minutes.

Meanwhile wipe the saucepan with some kitchen paper, then melt the butter in it and let the onion sweat very gently in the butter (without browning) for about 10 minutes. By that time the haddock will be ready, so remove it onto a board, reserving the liquid, and peel off the skin.

Next stir the flour into the onion and butter to soak up the juices, then gradually add the fish-cooking liquid, stirring as you do so. When it's all in, add half the haddock separated into flakes. Now pour the soup into the goblet of a liquidiser or food processor and blend thoroughly, then after that pass it all through a sieve back into the saucepan (pressing any solid bits of haddock to extract all the flavour). Discard what's left in the sieve, then add the remaining haddock separated into small flakes. Taste the soup, and season as required with salt, pepper and lemon juice.

Now bring it up to the gentlest possible simmer and simply break an egg into it. Because the liquid is not clear you won't be able to see the egg cooking, but don't panic – trust me! In about 4 minutes you can slip a draining spoon in and lift the egg up to see how it's cooking: a really soft poached egg should just about be ready, but you can give it longer if you like.

Sprinkle with chopped parsley and serve this in a shallow soup plate, so the poached egg can sit proudly in the centre. I like this with thinly sliced brown bread and butter.

Fresh tomato and courgette soup

This is a light soup, perfect for late summer when both courgettes and overripe tomatoes are cheap and plentiful.

8 oz red ripe tomatoes (225 g)
8 oz courgettes (225 g), sliced with their skins left on
1 small onion, chopped
1 dessertspoon olive oil
1 rounded teaspoon tomato purée
½ pint hot water (275 ml)
1 clove of garlic, peeled and chopped
½ teaspoon coriander seeds, crushed
⅓ teaspoon oregano
salt and freshly milled black pepper

Begin by pouring boiling water over the tomatoes. Then leave them for 5 minutes for the skins to loosen. Heat the oil in a medium-sized saucepan, add the onion and soften it for about 5 minutes. Next add the garlic, coriander and oregano and stir these around for a minute or two to allow the heat to draw out their flavour and aroma – the whole thing will soon begin to smell like a Greek kitchen!

Now skin and chop the tomatoes and add these to the pan along with the courgettes. Then, keeping the heat very low, put a lid on and let the vegetables sweat for about 10 minutes.

Next whisk the tomato purée into the hot water, pour this into the saucepan, stir and simmer gently (with the lid on) for a further 10 minutes. Finally, take the lid off and give the whole lot another 5 minutes cooking uncovered. Then whizz the soup to a purée in an electric blender, taste to check the seasoning, then reheat and serve either with garlic croûtons sprinkled over, or with some hot garlic bread.

Quick French onion soup

This is a winner. I promise you that you won't notice it hasn't been made by the traditional method with strongly reduced meat stock. The topping of crunchy garlic croûtons and bubbling melted cheese makes this a very warming soup for chilly winter's evenings.

8 oz onions (225 g), thinly sliced
1 tablespoon olive oil
1 level teaspoon granulated sugar
1 clove of garlic, crushed
½ pint stock or hot water (275 ml)
¼ pint dry white wine or dry cider (150 ml)
1 tablespoon mushroom ketchup
1½ heaped tablespoons garlic croûtons
¾ oz Gruyère or strong Cheddar cheese (20 g), grated
salt and freshly milled black pepper

Heat the oil in a medium-sized saucepan until it's sizzling hot, then add the onions (it will look as if you've got too much, but don't worry – they will collapse considerably). Sprinkle in the sugar but don't stir too soon – let the onions touching the heat get brown for about 1 minute. Then stir, and leave again, repeating this until all the edges of the onion have turned a dark caramel brown. The sugar will help to achieve this.

Now add the garlic, let that cook for a minute or two, then add the stock, wine and mushroom ketchup and season with salt and pepper. Give it all a good stir, then turn the heat down to a very gentle simmer, and simmer for 15 minutes.

While that's happening, preheat the grill to its highest setting. When the soup is ready pour it into a fireproof bowl, scatter the croûtons on top (piling them up a little bit) and sprinkle the cheese over. Place the bowl under the grill until the cheese is brown and bubbling. This is good served with warm crusty French bread – which can be warmed while the grill is preheating.

Leek and lentil soup

Whole green or brown lentils have a lovely fragrant flavour – and don't need long soaking. They make a perfect partner to leeks in this thick, creamy soup.

1 medium leek, washed and trimmed, but leave some of the green part
1 oz whole green or brown lentils (25 g)
1 rasher lean bacon, chopped
6 fl oz water or stock (175 ml)
½ oz butter (10 g)
2 fl oz milk (55 ml)
an extra ¼ pint water (150 ml)
freshly grated nutmeg
salt and freshly milled black pepper

For the garnish: 1 tablespoon of raw leek or spring onion

First of all put the lentils in a small saucepan and pour in 6 fl oz (175 ml) of water or stock. Cover them and simmer gently for 40 minutes.

Meanwhile split the leeks lengthways then cut them up crossways fairly finely. Now in another saucepan heat the butter and add the chopped bacon followed by the leeks. Put a lid on and leave them to sweat gently for about 15 minutes – checking now and then to make sure they're not catching on the bottom.

When the lentils have had their time, add the leek and bacon (and the buttery juice) to them, pour in the milk and top up with the extra ¼ pint (150 ml) of water. Season with salt, pepper and a good grating of nutmeg. Cover the pan and continue to simmer gently for another 20 minutes.

After that liquidise the soup in a blender or food processor, return it to the pan to reheat, taste, and season if necessary, and thin down with more milk if you think it needs it. This is nice served with some chopped raw leek or spring onion as a garnish. Serve with crusty wholemeal bread.

Brown kidney soup

A warming, comforting soup, this one, for when you've had a hard day. It's quick to prepare and will simmer away happily for an hour while you unwind with a relaxing bath and after that sip sherry with your feet up!

6 oz ox kidney (175 g)
¾ pint hot stock or water (425 ml)
1 dessertspoon mushroom ketchup
½ teaspoon tomato purée
1 teaspoon Worcestershire sauce
1 oz butter (25 g)
1 small onion, chopped
1 rounded dessertspoon plain flour
1 sprig of thyme or ¼ teaspoon dried thyme
1 bayleaf
2 tablespoons dry sherry
salt and freshly milled black pepper

For the garnish: croûtons

Trim off all the fleshy parts from the ox kidney and chop them up fairly small. Now put the tough core of the kidney into a saucepan, add the hot stock or water and boil with a lid on for 10 minutes. After that discard the kidney core and to the stock add the mushroom ketchup, tomato purée and Worcestershire sauce. Pour all this into a jug.

Now wipe out the saucepan with kitchen paper, then melt the fat in it and first soften the onion – allowing it to brown a little round the edges. Next turn the heat right up and add the kidney pieces and let them brown nicely as you move them around the pan.

After that sprinkle in the flour and thyme, stir to soak up all the juices, then gradually add the stock a little at a time, stirring well after each addition. Now add the bayleaf and some seasoning, then cover and simmer the soup over the gentlest possible heat for 1 hour. Add the sherry just before serving, and allow it to come back to a simmer. Serve very hot with croûtons as a garnish.

Thick celery soup with smoked bacon

For vegetarians – or simply for a change – it is a nice idea to omit the bacon and pile some croûtons on top of this soup in a heatproof bowl, then sprinkle with ³⁄₄ oz (20 g) of strong Cheddar and melt under a hot grill.

2 medium sticks of celery, chopped fairly small
2 oz chopped leek (50 g)
1 small potato, peeled and chopped
1 oz butter or alternative (25 g)
7 fl oz hot water or stock (200 ml)
2 small rashers of smoked streaky bacon
salt and freshly milled black pepper

For the garnish: croûtons

First of all melt the butter in a thick-based saucepan, then add the leek, celery and potato. Stir them around to get a nice coating of butter and add some salt and pepper. Now put a lid on. Keeping the heat very low, allow them to sweat gently for 10–15 minutes.

After that, pour in the stock or water. Stir again, pop the lid back on and simmer gently for a further 10–15 minutes or until the vegetables are soft. Meanwhile preheat the grill, and cook the bacon rashers until they are crisp enough to be crumbled up into little bits.

Next blend the soup to a purée in a liquidiser or food processor, and after that pass it through a sieve (in case there are any fibrous bits left in the celery). Return to the pan to reheat and taste to check the seasoning. Finally stir in the crumbled pieces of bacon. Serve very hot, garnished, if you like, with some plain croûtons.

Curried vegetable soup with brown rice

This soup is fresh, tangy and unusual. Yet it can be made from those slightly tired-looking salad vegetables that lurk unused in the fridge.

6 oz cucumber (175 g), peeled and chopped
3 medium tomatoes
1 small potato, chopped
4 outside lettuce leaves, shredded
½ medium onion, chopped small
¼ cupful long-grain brown rice
1 oz butter or margarine (25 g)
½ teaspoon Madras curry powder
1 rounded teaspoon tomato purée
½ teaspoon Worcestershire sauce
8 fl oz stock or water (225 ml)
a squeeze of lemon juice
salt and freshly milled black pepper

For the garnish: wholemeal garlic croûtons and finely chopped spring-onion top

First put the rice on: with a small quantity like this, use your smallest saucepan and add ¾ teacupful of boiling water and ½ teaspoon of salt. Simmer very gently for 30 minutes.

Meanwhile pour boiling water over the tomatoes and leave them to soak for 5 minutes to loosen their skins. Next heat the butter in a medium saucepan and soften the onion in it for 5 minutes before adding the cucumber, lettuce, potato, skinned tomatoes and curry powder. Stir everything around, breaking up the tomatoes, with a wooden spoon. Season with salt and pepper, then put a lid on and let the vegetables sweat over a gentle heat for 10 minutes.

While that's happening mix the tomato purée and Worcestershire sauce with the stock (or water) then pour this over the vegetables in the pan and bring back up to simmering point. Next in a liquidiser or food processor, blend everything almost to a purée – but not too smooth, leave a little texture to the vegetables.

Now return it to the saucepan, and as soon as the rice has had its 30 minutes tip it (and any remaining water) into the soup, and simmer gently for a further 10 minutes without a lid. Taste to check the seasoning and add the lemon juice and a couple more pinches of curry powder if you like it a little more spicy. Serve with wholemeal garlic croûtons and, if you have any, a little finely chopped spring-onion top.

Thick cheese and onion soup

This is a good stomach-warmer – ideal if you're suffering from a cold or the after-effects of flu and you need something comforting!

1 medium onion, chopped small
1 oz butter (25 g)
¾ oz flour (20 g)
6 fl oz milk (175 ml)
6 fl oz stock or water (175 ml)
2 fl oz single cream (55 ml)
¾ oz strong Cheddar cheese (20 g), grated
freshly grated nutmeg
salt and freshly milled black pepper

For the garnish: Parmesan croûtons (see page 38)

Melt the butter in a medium-sized saucepan and sweat the onion in it over a low heat (with the lid on) for about 15 minutes. Then stir in the flour and blend well to soak up all the buttery onion juices and make a smooth paste.

Now gradually add the milk and stock, stirring well after each addition and finishing off with a whisk to make sure everything is smooth and lump-free. Now turn the heat to the lowest possible simmer and let it barely simmer for about 6 minutes. Just before serving stir in the cream and grated cheese – leave it on the heat for a minute or so, but don't let it boil. Season with salt, pepper and freshly grated nutmeg, then serve sprinkled with Parmesan croûtons.

Thick peasant soup with barley

You need to be quite hungry for this one, because (as its name might imply) it's hefty and substantial.

1 small carrot
1 medium onion
1 leek, cleaned
a 3 inch piece of celery (7·5 cm)
1 heaped tablespoon pearl barley
1 teaspoon tomato purée
¾ pint hot stock or water (425 ml)
1 oz butter (25 g)
1 small clove of garlic, crushed
1 tablespoon cream
salt and freshly milled black pepper

For the garnish: chopped parsley, and serve with sesame toast (see page 39)

Start off by whisking the tomato purée into the hot water or stock, then pour this into a medium-sized saucepan along with the pearl barley. Bring up to simmering point and simmer gently for about 40 minutes or until the barley is tender.

Meanwhile chop all the vegetables very finely (as the pieces are going to be left whole and not liquidised, they do need to start off quite small). Ten minutes before the barley is ready, melt the butter in another saucepan then stir all the prepared vegetables into it together with the garlic so they get a good coating of fat, then season with salt and pepper, turn the heat down to low, put a lid on and leave the vegetables to sweat to draw out the juices for about 10 minutes.

When you take the lid off the fresh aroma is fantastic! Now add the barley and stock to the vegetables and continue to simmer the lot (covered) for a further 10 minutes. Stir in the cream just before serving, and serve very hot with the parsley sprinkled over and with the sesame toast.

Creamy mushroom soup

This is a light and delicate soup that is best made with the dark, flat open-gilled mushrooms – which have more flavour to them than the closed button variety.

4 oz dark open mushrooms (110 g)
1 oz butter (25 g)
1 small onion, finely chopped
1 tablespoon dry sherry
grated whole nutmeg
5 fl oz milk (150 ml)
5 fl oz stock or water (150 ml)
1 dessertspoon mushroom ketchup
1 dessertspoon lemon juice
1 tablespoon single cream
salt and freshly milled black pepper

For the garnish: 2 small mushrooms, thinly sliced

First of all wipe the mushrooms with some damp kitchen paper if they need it. Melt the butter in a medium-sized saucepan and soften the onion in it over a medium heat for about 5 minutes. Then chop the mushrooms fairly small and add them to the pan along with the sherry. Stir well, season with salt and pepper and a little grated nutmeg, then lower the heat, put a lid on and leave for 5 minutes for the heat to draw out the mushroom juice.

Next add the milk, stock and mushroom ketchup, stir and simmer again with the lid on for 10 minutes. After that transfer half the soup to a blender and whizz to a purée, then return it to the saucepan along with the lemon juice. Taste to check the seasoning, then reheat gently, adding the cream just before serving. Garnish with slices of raw mushroom.

Minestrone with macaroni

This is a very filling, satisfying soup that needs to be served in a deep, wide soup plate so there's plenty of room to sprinkle lots of Parmesan cheese over.

1 leek (2 oz, 50 g)
½ stick of celery
1 small carrot (1 oz, 25 g)
1 medium courgette
1 largish ripe red tomato
1 small onion
1 clove of garlic, chopped
2 rashers of streaky bacon
1 dessertspoon olive oil
1 dessertspoon tomato purée
12 fl oz stock or hot water (330 ml)
½ teaspoon dried basil or 1 teaspoon fresh chopped basil
1 oz short-cut macaroni or any of the other small pasta shapes (25 g)
1 dessertspoon fresh chopped parsley
salt and freshly milled black pepper

First pour some boiling water over the tomatoes, then after a couple of minutes skin them and chop the flesh roughly. Cut the leek almost in half lengthways and fan it out under a running tap to get rid of any grit and dust. Now chop all the vegetables fairly finely, and take the rind off the bacon and chop that finely as well.

Now heat up the oil in a largish saucepan and fry the onion, garlic and bacon in it for 5 minutes to soften. Then add the celery, carrot and tomato, stir these into the oil and juices, add some salt and pepper, then turn the heat to low, cover the pan and leave the vegetables and bacon to sweat for about 10 minutes.

Meanwhile mix the tomato purée with the hot stock or water and stir in the dried basil (if you're lucky enough to have fresh basil, put that in only at the very end). After the ten minutes are up, pour in the stock and gently simmer the soup (with a lid on) for 30 minutes, stirring once or twice during that time.

After that add the leeks and courgettes to the soup, bring back to simmering point, then add the pasta and continue simmering gently, uncovered now, for a further 15 minutes. Stir in the parsley before serving the soup (with lots of Parmesan sprinkled over).

Red bean and pasta soup

This is what I would call a storecupboard soup – for the days when the refrigerator is unyielding and there is no time to shop

1 small tin of red kidney beans (7½ oz, 215 g)
1 oz small-cut macaroni or pasta shells (25 g)
½ small onion, chopped
1 tablespoon olive oil
1 small clove of garlic, crushed
1 teaspoon fresh or dried basil
1 rounded dessertspoon tomato purée
12 fl oz hot water (330 ml)
salt and freshly milled black pepper

For the garnish: 1 tablespoon freshly grated Parmesan

The first and most important step is to empty the beans into a sieve and give them a thorough rinsing under the cold tap (to rid them of the sugary liquid they are preserved in). Next heat the oil in a medium-sized saucepan, then stir in the onion and garlic and soften them to the pale-gold stage.

After that, add the beans and the basil, stirring these around in the oil. Mix the tomato purée into the hot water, pour this in, then cover the pan with a lid and simmer gently for 10 minutes.

Next ladle half the soup into the goblet of a blender and blend to a smooth purée before returning it to the other half. Now bring back to simmering point, add the pasta and a seasoning of salt and pepper, and simmer without a lid for 10 minutes. Serve very hot, sprinkled with Parmesan cheese.

Croûtons

If you want to make soup into a complete meal, some crisp bread croûtons will add just the right finishing touch. The best way to prepare them, I find, is to bake them in the oven: do this in one large batch, then when they've cooled they can be stored in a screwtop jar and will keep very crisp for up to two weeks.

Plain croûtons
(for 4 servings – see above)

2 oz bread cut into small cubes (50 g), this can be white or wholewheat

1 tablespoon olive oil

Preheat the oven to gas mark 4, 350°F, 180°C

Spoon the olive oil onto a small baking-sheet, then using the back of a tablespoon spread it out evenly over the baking-sheet. Now arrange the cubes of bread on the sheet and stir them around to soak up the oil, turning them over as well, so that they get an even coating.

Then bake them in the oven for 10 minutes or until they are crisp and golden-brown. One word of warning: do use a kitchen timer for this operation because it's actually very hard to bake something for just 10 minutes without forgetting all about it. I have baked more batches of charcoal-coloured croûtons than I care to remember!

Garlic croûtons

For these you use the same recipe as above, only this time you spread one crushed clove of garlic over the baking-sheet along with the oil.

Parmesan croûtons

These are so good I usually eat most of them before even thinking of making soup. The method for these is slightly different: here you place the oil and the cubes of bread in a small bowl, stir them around to soak up the oil, and then sprinkle in 1 dessertspoon of freshly grated Parmesan. Stir the cubes around to coat them in that as well, then spread them on the baking-sheet and bake as above.

Sesame toast

Cut up into 'fingers' this goes well with several of the soups in this chapter, and also with some of the egg dishes in the next chapter (i.e. scrambled eggs with smoked salmon). To make one slice you need:

1 medium-cut slice from a large loaf or its equivalent
butter
1 teaspoon sesame seeds

Preheat the grill, and toast the slice of bread on one side only. Then butter it on the untoasted side (right up to the edges) and sprinkle the sesame seeds all over it to cover as evenly as possible, pressing them down so they will stay in position (if you're lucky). Return the bread to the grill. Toast the sesame-encrusted side until the sesame seeds are lightly toasted and the bread itself golden-brown. Then cut the slice up into four fingers and eat straightaway.

Simply Eggs

One is fun!

Personally I have a particular fondness for egg dishes. If I find myself eating alone these, more often than not, are what I choose to eat – maybe because I'm not a breakfast person and have missed out on them earlier in the day! One of their more useful attributes is that they are actually faster than most (if not all) so-called fast foods. Look, as I did while preparing this chapter, along the instant-meal shelves in any supermarket and see how much reheating etc most of the items require: eggs on the other hand take only minutes.

I've had great fun in this chapter finding alternatives to oven-cooked eggs. Preheating an oven for half a dozen eggs en cocotte may be justified, but one in a large oven looks very lonely! It's been interesting to discover how well en cocotte dishes can be 'baked' on top of the stove – and grilling eggs has been a completely new experience for me.

Freshness is important, of course, in all areas of cooking, but especially so with eggs. So do try to buy yours from a shop or supermarket that you know has a large turnover, and always keep a close eye on the date-stamp on the carton. Should you find – as we all do – that one or two eggs have been lurking about rather longer than they should, the best idea is to separate them and use the yolk for quick mayonnaise (*see page 172*) and the white for leek fritters (*see page 179*).

Swiss baked eggs

This is another little gem of a supper dish for one, and it's made in moments. Serve it with fingers of wholewheat toast. Although you can use other cheeses, it's really best made with Gruyère.

2 large eggs
2 dessertspoons cream
1 oz Gruyère cheese (25 g) grated
salt and freshly milled black pepper

A 3 inch (7.5 cm) ramekin, buttered

First you need a medium-sized saucepan, with a lid, that is big enough to hold the ramekin and leave enough space round it for you to lift it in and out. So place the dish in the saucepan and pour in enough water to come two-thirds of the way up the side of the ramekin. Put the saucepan on to heat and allow the water to come up to simmering point.

While you're waiting, pour 1 dessertspoon of cream into the base of the dish to heat through. Now break two eggs into the ramekin, season them with salt and pepper, then put a lid on the saucepan and let it simmer very gently for 6–7 minutes or until the eggs are just set.

Meanwhile preheat the grill, then when the eggs are ready carefully remove the ramekin from the pan (using a cloth to protect your hands). Spoon the rest of the cream over the eggs then sprinkle with the grated cheese, and place the dish under a very hot grill for a few seconds until the cheese bubbles. Then serve straightaway.

Note: these timings will give a firm set to the eggs. If you want them softer just give them five minutes' simmering.

Cheese soufflé omelette

If you're not an experienced cook, you need a bit of courage for this one. It's not at all difficult, it's just that it often looks as if it's not going to work. But it always does and it's absolutely delightful.

2 large eggs
2 oz grated cheese (50 g) (you can use any kind of cheese you like, but I happen to like this with Double Gloucester or Cheddar with Onion and Chives)
½ oz (10 g) butter
1 tablespoon freshly grated Parmesan
salt and freshly milled black pepper

First of all preheat the grill. Then separate the eggs, putting the whites in a large roomy bowl and the yolks in a smaller one. Before you begin to whisk put a heavy-based 7-inch frying-pan onto a medium heat.

Now take an electric hand-whisk (or other kind) and whisk the egg whites to the soft-peak stage (i.e. when you lift the whisk up the egg white forms soft peaks that droop over slightly). Using the same whisk, whisk the egg yolks for a few seconds and add a little salt and pepper. Then pop the butter into the pan to melt and meanwhile, using a metal tablespoon, fold the egg yolks into the whites and when they're evenly incorporated fold in the grated cheese.

By now the butter should be hot so pour the mixture into the pan, and shake the pan to distribute the mixture evenly but don't do anything else like stirring – you'll just have to leave it alone for about one minute. Then you can slide a palette knife round the edge to loosen it.

Sprinkle the surface of the omelette with half the Parmesan, then take the pan over to the grill and let the surface cook for another minute or until it begins to be faintly tinged with brown. Have a warm plate ready, then once again slide the palette knife all round the edge of the omelette. Slip it underneath and turn the omelette right over in half and tip out onto the plate (if it flips back, just turn it over again). Sprinkle with the rest of the Parmesan and eat immediately. It won't wait.

Cheese soufflé omelette with spinach filling

For this you prepare in advance 2 oz (50 g) of frozen spinach, cooked with a knob of butter and finished with a dessertspoon of cream and some pepper and salt. Spoon the spinach onto one side of the cooked omelette before serving.

Cheese soufflé omelette with bacon filling

Fry (or grill) 1 oz (25 g) of chopped bacon till crisp. Transfer it to a plate and fold it into the beaten eggs along with the cheese.

Scrambled eggs with cream cheese and herbs

This can be made with any cream cheese flavoured with garlic and herbs (Boursin is probably the best known of this kind), and the combination produces a wonderfully creamy consistency. In the summer a dessertspoon of fresh snipped chives will make it even better. Serve on thick, well toasted wholewheat bread.

2 large eggs (or 3 if you're ravenous)
½ oz butter (10 g)
1½ oz Boursin or any cream cheese with garlic and herbs (40 g)
salt and freshly milled black pepper

First break the eggs into a bowl and whisk them together with a good seasoning of salt and pepper.

Then in a medium-sized saucepan melt the butter and when it's hot swirl it around to coat the base and sides of the pan. Now pour in the eggs and, using a wooden spoon, stir like mad getting the edge of the spoon right into the corner of the pan to prevent the egg there setting too fast.

In about 30 seconds you will have half solid and half liquid eggs – take the pan off the heat and crumble in the Boursin in smallish pieces. Now back onto the heat and more furious stirring till you have a lovely creamy mass with no liquid egg left. Serve straightaway.

Scrambled eggs with smoked salmon

This sounds more extravagant than it is. In fact it makes very little smoked salmon go a long way, and can be made with salmon offcuts or a couple of slices taken from a frozen pack if you have one in the freezer. It's simplicity itself, but the creaminess of the eggs and the smokiness of the salmon make this a four-star meal for one.

2 large eggs
2 oz smoked salmon (50 g)
2 tablespoons milk
1 oz butter (25 g)
salt and freshly milled black pepper

Serve with: either triangles of fried bread, buttered wholemeal toast, sesame toast (see page 39) *or simply slices of brown bread and butter*

Begin by chopping the smoked salmon reasonably small, then put it into a mug or cup and pour the milk over it. Stir well so that all the salmon gets a good coating of milk, then leave it on one side for about 20 minutes.

After that melt ½ oz (10 g) butter in a small heavy saucepan, then break the eggs into a bowl and beat them well, seasoning with salt and pepper. When the butter is foaming swirl it around to coat the sides of the pan, then pour in the beaten eggs. Now, with a wooden spoon, stir continuously, getting right into the corner of the pan. Soon the eggs will begin to solidify and when you have about 50% solid and the rest liquid, add the salmon (which will by now have absorbed all the milk). Keep stirring like mad, and when almost all the liquid has gone remove the pan from the heat, add the remaining ½ oz (10 g) of butter and continue stirring. The eggs will finish cooking to a creamy mass in the heat of the pan. Taste to check the seasoning, then serve straightaway.

Scrambled eggs with bacon and mushrooms

You could either serve this with a large, thick slice of buttered wholemeal toast, or you could pile it into a gratin dish and serve with triangles of crisp fried wholemeal bread. Dark-gilled mushrooms tend to spoil the colour a little, so it's best to use button mushrooms.

2 large eggs
2 rashers of bacon
2 oz button mushrooms (50 g)
approx 1 oz butter (25 g)
salt and freshly milled black pepper

First fry the bacon in a little butter until it's fairly crisp, then remove it to a warmed serving dish and chop it up quite small, and keep it warm.

Next fry the mushrooms in the bacon fat, tossing them around the pan and only cooking them very lightly. Then remove them and add them to the bacon. Now take a saucepan and melt about ½ oz (10 g) of butter in it. Whisk the eggs together in a basin, season them with salt and pepper, then stir them into the butter, using a wooden spoon – keep stirring over a medium heat and scrape the base (and especially the corners) of the pan to prevent the eggs sticking.

When they are half cooked (i.e. about half cooked egg and half liquid) remove the saucepan from the heat, add another knob of butter, then stir until the butter has melted and the eggs (which will go on cooking in the heat of the pan) are soft and glossy. Now mix in the mushroom and bacon, and pile the mixture onto toast or into a gratin dish.

Slimmer's scramble

This is another scrambled-egg recipe, but unlike the preceding ones it is perfect for diet days. It needs to be cooked in a non-stick pan, but even with the best non-stick equipment I prefer to moisten it first. So for this recipe I use a very small quantity – less than half a teaspoon – of St Ivel Gold, which has half the calories of butter or margarine. Just swirl it round the preheated pan and, if necessary, drain off any excess before adding the eggs.

2 large eggs
1 heaped dessertspoon cottage cheese
2 spring onions, finely chopped
salt and freshly milled black pepper
2 slices wholewheat toast

Begin by whisking the eggs in a bowl and add the salt, pepper and spring onions to them. Now preheat the non-stick saucepan and moisten it as described in the introduction. Next add the beaten eggs then, using a wooden spoon, start to scramble them by stirring quickly, getting right into the corners of the pan – all this over a medium heat.

When the eggs are still half set and half liquid, add the cottage cheese and continue to scramble vigorously, removing the pan from the heat before they are actually set – they will go on cooking on the way to the toast! Spread the toast with the merest trace of Gold, top with the fluffy creamy eggs and serve immediately.

Eggs and leek en cocotte

Although traditionally eggs are baked individually in cocotte dishes in the oven and served as a first course, for a fairly substantial supper dish you can, instead, cook two of them in a larger ramekin on top of the stove, finishing them off under the grill.

2 large eggs
2 leeks, trimmed
1 oz butter or alternative (25 g)
4 tablespoons single cream
1 oz grated Gruyère cheese or Cheddar (25 g) or alternatively, 2 tablespoons grated Parmesan cheese
salt and freshly milled black pepper

You'll also need a buttered 4 inch (10 cm) ramekin dish

First of all clean the leeks by slitting them almost in two lengthways then fanning them out under a cold tap to get rid of any grit lodged between the layers. Then dry them with kitchen paper, slice them completely in half, and then cut them across into ½ inch (1 cm) slices.

Now in a small saucepan melt the butter, add the leeks and over a gentle heat (to prevent them colouring) cook them for about 6 minutes or until they're soft. Then transfer them to the base of the ramekin and spread them out evenly.

Next, carefully break the eggs in on top, season them with salt and freshly milled pepper, then spoon the cream in on top. To cook them, pour about an inch of boiling water into a saucepan wide enough to place the ramekin inside. Bring the water back to a simmer, then lower the ramekin in, put a lid on the pan and simmer very gently for 10–15 minutes (depending on how you like your eggs cooked). While that's happening, preheat the grill. Finally remove the ramekin from the pan (using a cloth to hold it), sprinkle the cheese on top and place under the grill for a further 4–5 minutes. Serve as soon as they're ready – with thinly sliced wholemeal bread and butter.

Omelette with creamed mushrooms

The filling for this omelette is a traditional French mushroom stuffing called duxelles, *which with a little cream or yoghurt added makes this particular omelette distinctly different.*

2 large eggs
3 oz dark, open mushrooms (75 g)
2 oz onion (50 g), approx 1 small onion
1½ oz butter or alternative (40 g)
1 dessertspoon olive oil
1 dessertspoon fresh yoghurt or cream
freshly grated nutmeg
salt and freshly milled black pepper

Begin by chopping the mushrooms as finely as possible, and do the same with the onion. Then melt half the butter with the oil in a small saucepan, stir in the onion and allow it to cook for 5 minutes before stirring in the chopped mushrooms. Continue to cook the mixture over a gentle heat (without a lid) for about 20–25 minutes, so that the juices will be drawn out of the onion and mushrooms and evaporate, leaving a concentrated mixture. Now season with salt, pepper and a little freshly grated nutmeg.

Now to make the omelette. Melt the rest of the butter in a 7 inch (18 cm) frying-pan and swirl it round to coat the pan. Then lightly mix two eggs and season them with salt and pepper. At this stage stir the cream or yoghurt into the *duxelles* mixture.

When the butter is foaming hot pour the eggs in and spoon the mushroom mixture along the centre of the egg mixture. Draw the cooked edges into the centre of the pan then tip it to allow the liquid egg to reach the sides. As soon as the omelette is set, flip one side over to the centre, and tip out onto a warmed plate, folding over the remaining half as you turn it out.

Omelette Mère Poulard

This famous omelette comes from Mont St Michel in Normandy. Mère Poulard, who died in 1931, used to make this omelette every night at her hotel – and there are two restaurants now in Mont St Michel who claim to be her true heirs. I have eaten it at one of them: whether it was authentic, I don't know, but it was delicious, fluffy, melting in the mouth and made in moments.

2 large eggs
½ teaspoon butter
1 dessertspoon olive oil
salt and freshly milled black pepper

You must use olive oil to get a nice light crisp base to the omelette. So start by melting the butter and oil together in a 7 inch (18 cm) thick-based frying-pan, and while that's happening break the eggs into a large bowl and add a seasoning of salt and freshly milled pepper.

Now take an electric hand-whisk (or a rotary or balloon whisk) and whisk the eggs for 1 to 1½ minutes or until they have changed to a paler colour and have taken on a rather thick, mousse-like texture. At this stage turn on the grill to preheat.

Next take hold of the frying-pan and swirl the oil all round the edges, then as soon as the fat is very hot, pour in the eggs. Shake the pan but don't do any stirring at all – just leave it for a few seconds to set underneath. Then take a palette knife and lift the edge of the omelette just to take a peep and make sure it's golden. I find that a minute's cooking on top of the stove is sufficient.

Now place the frying-pan under the grill and continue to cook there for another minute to set the top. Have a heated plate ready and, using the palette knife, flip the edge over as if to fold it in half (though hopefully it will be too fluffy to fold in half completely!) and slide the omelette out on to the plate, and serve straightaway.

Omelette Parmentier

The above is the French name for potato omelette, but it could equally be called a tortilla or Spanish omelette. The thing they all have in common is that they're served flat and not folded like the classical French omelette. Turning them over in the pan to cook the other side is a hazardous affair – and requires a skill I have not entirely mastered. I therefore concede humbly to hanging on to my serenity by switching on the grill.

Note: if you like, you could sprinkle some grated cheese on this before it goes to the grill. And of course you can use other fillings, like chopped green pepper, chopped leek, chopped bacon ... the variations are endless.

2 or 3 eggs
6 oz potatoes (175 g), peeled weight
2 spring onions, finely chopped – the green parts as well
1 dessertspoon olive oil
salt and freshly milled black pepper

For this you need a solid 7 inch (18 cm) (diameter) frying-pan. Also preheat the grill before you start.

Now slice the potatoes, then cut the slices into strips like chips and cut the strips across – so you end up with small cubes. Heat the oil in the frying-pan and while it's heating, pat the potato cubes as dry as you can in a clean tea-cloth.

When the oil is very hot add the potato and toss it around the pan to colour around the edges, then turn the heat down to medium and let the potatoes go on cooking for 10 minutes. Add the spring onions and cook for a further minute or two.

Break the eggs into a bowl, season with salt and pepper and beat them lightly. Now increase the heat to full under the pan, pour the eggs in then, using a palette knife, draw the outside of the omelette inwards and tip the pan to let the liquid egg run to the edges all round.

When the underside of the omelette looks set and there's only about half the liquid egg left on top, take the omelette pan to the grill and set it underneath to allow the heat of the grill to cook the top – not for too long because the omelette needs to be a little moist in the centre. Serve immediately (with an interesting salad).

Omelette Lorraine

I've come to the conclusion that a Quiche Lorraine for one is too much of a fiddle (especially as Marks & Spencer do delicious individual quiches). However you can capture that Alsace Lorraine combination of eggs, cheese and bacon in this omelette instead.

2 large eggs
1 rasher smoked bacon (1 oz, 25 g), chopped
1 oz leek (25 g), chopped
1 oz Gruyère cheese (25 g), grated
½ oz butter (10 g)
salt and freshly milled black pepper

You'll need a 7 inch (18 cm) heavy-based frying-pan for this and you begin by melting half the butter in it. Add the chopped bacon and cook it for 5 minutes or until the fat starts to run from it. Then add the leek and stir everything around. Put a lid on the pan and keep the heat low while you let the leek soften for 5 minutes.

Meanwhile heat up the grill. Break the eggs into a bowl, season them with salt and pepper – not too much salt because of the bacon – then beat them lightly. When the leek has softened use a draining spoon to remove it (and the bacon) to a plate and keep on one side. Now turn the heat right up, add the rest of the butter to the pan and when it is hot and foaming, pour in the eggs quickly followed by the bacon and leek sprinkled over and then by the cheese (also sprinkled over).

Draw the edges of the omelette inwards a little, and tip the pan to allow almost all the liquid egg to get to the edges. Then take the whole thing to the hot grill and grill for a few seconds until the cheese has melted. Have a warmed plate ready: tip the pan and flip the outer edge of the omelette to the centre, then turn it over again as you ease it onto the plate. Serve with fresh bread and a plain lettuce salad.

Frittata with spinach and cheese

This is an open-faced omelette from Italy that is served flat and not folded like a French omelette. In fact the normal rules of omelette-making can be ignored for this because, instead of needing swift handling and high heat, it is cooked slowly over a low heat.

2 large or 3 smaller eggs
1 large spring onion, finely chopped
½ lb fresh spinach (225 g) or ¼ lb (110 g) frozen spinach defrosted, well drained and chopped
freshly grated nutmeg
olive oil
1 tablespoon freshly grated Parmesan cheese
salt and freshly milled black pepper

If you're using fresh spinach, prepare it by washing it in several changes of cold water to remove all the dust, then tear the leaves away and discard the stalks. Drain the leaves by shaking them in a colander then pile them into a thick-based saucepan with some salt and a knob of butter. Then put a lid on and cook the spinach, giving the pan a good shake now and then: the cooking time will vary, but it shouldn't take more than a minute or two.

Meanwhile soften the onion with a little butter in a thick-based frying-pan – for just half a minute or so. Then when the spinach is cooked, drain it thoroughly in the colander, pressing out all the excess juice. Then chop it finely and add it to the onion along with a seasoning of freshly grated nutmeg.

Next return the pan with about a dessertspoon of olive oil to the very lowest heat possible (if this is not very low it might be advisable to use a cooling mat). Now break the eggs into a bowl, stir them lightly with a fork to amalgamate them, then add the chopped spinach and onion to the eggs with half a tablespoon of Parmesan and some seasoning.

Swirl the oil all round the pan, then pour in the egg mixture and just leave it, without stirring, on that very low heat for 10–15 minutes. Meanwhile preheat the grill. Ease up one edge of the omelette with a palette knife to make sure it is golden underneath, then transfer the pan to sit under the grill to set the top. Sprinkle with the rest of the Parmesan and serve immediately.

Gratinée of eggs Savoyard

This is one of my favourites if I'm cooking just for myself. It takes just thirty minutes to prepare and needs nothing else other than some crusty French bread, good butter – and perhaps a glass of something as well.

2 large eggs
6 oz potato (175 g), peeled weight
2 rashers of bacon (approx 2 oz, 50 g), chopped small
1 medium onion, chopped
1 tablespoon olive oil
1½ oz grated cheese (40 g)
salt and freshly milled black pepper

Begin by chopping the potato into ¼ inch (5 mm) dice, then dry them as thoroughly as possible in a clean tea-towel. Now in a thick heavy 7 inch (18 cm) frying-pan heat the oil to very hot then add the potato (standing well back as it will splutter on contact with oil). Now give them 1 minute to brown a little before turning them over to let the other side brown. Then turn the heat to medium and let the potatoes cook for 10 minutes more, moving them around the pan now and then.

After that add the bacon and onion and cook for a further 10 minutes (still stirring from time to time). While that's going on, preheat the grill and prepare a heatproof gratin dish (9 inches × 5½ inches, 23 × 14 cm) by oiling the inside. When the contents of the frying-pan are ready, arrange them over the base of the dish, making two depressions with the back of a tablespoon, and add a seasoning of pepper (but no salt – because of the bacon).

Now break the two eggs into the depressions, season them with salt and pepper, then sprinkle the grated cheese all over and grill – about 3–4 inches away from the heat – for about 7 minutes for soft-set eggs or 10 minutes for hard. Serve straightaway.

Eggs baked in smoked haddock

A simple supper dish, which you could make more substantial by putting a rim of hot creamed potato round the edge of a buttered 9 inch (23 cm) gratin dish, then spooning the smoked haddock etc. into the centre.

6 oz smoked haddock (175 g)
1 bayleaf
8 fl oz milk (225 ml)
¾ oz butter (20 g)
1 rounded dessertspoon flour
freshly grated nutmeg
1 large egg
1 oz grated Cheddar cheese (25 g)
a pinch of cayenne
salt and freshly milled black pepper

Place the smoked haddock, bayleaf and milk in a saucepan, cover with a lid, bring the milk up to simmering point then simmer gently for about 2 minutes. After that strain the milk into a jug, transfer the fish to a plate and remove (and discard) the skin. You can also throw out the bayleaf.

Now in the same saucepan melt the butter, then stir in the flour and when it's smooth and glossy gradually pour in the reserved milk, bit by bit, stirring all the time until you have a smooth sauce. Let the sauce simmer for 5 minutes and meanwhile preheat the grill. Next flake the haddock and add it to the sauce, cooking for a few minutes until it has reheated. Season with salt, pepper and some freshly grated nutmeg.

Now pour the hot mixture into a heatproof gratin dish, make a depression in the centre of the mixture (with the back of a tablespoon), then break the egg into this depression. Season with salt and pepper, then cover with the grated cheese and sprinkle with a good pinch of cayenne. Place the dish under the grill for 6–8 minutes or until the egg has set and the sauce is brown and bubbling. If you're not having creamed potatoes, serve with wholemeal bread and butter.

Fun Fish

Plaice fillets gratinée

Foil-baked salmon with dill and cucumber sauce

Chilled salmon with tarragon sauce

Portuguese baked fish

Goujons of lemon sole with herbs

Cheese-crusted fish pie

Fried herrings in oatmeal and crushed pepper

Foil-baked fish with lemon sauce

Provençale crusted cod with Provençale tomatoes

Poached fish with gherkin and caper sauce

Kedgeree with kippers

Prawns in chilli sauce

Salmon and caper fish cakes

Chilled marinated trout with pepper and tomatoes

Kashmir spiced prawns

Gratinée of prawns with avocado

Grilled trout with garlic, lemon and caper sauce

Plaice fillets tartare

Crab and mushrooms au gratin

One is fun!

For a long time I have been lamenting the decline in the number of high-street fishmongers (a strange phenomenon for a country completely surrounded by the sea), and things show no sign of improving. However I *am* more heartened by the advent of packaged fresh fish in chain stores and supermarkets. Marks & Spencer, for instance, always have a good selection which includes Dover sole, lemon sole, plaice, haddock and cod along with fresh farmed trout and salmon. What's more they all seem to be available in single-sized portions.

Fish has so very much to recommend it to the single cook (not least in these days when the nutritionist and heart specialist point the finger at the excessive amount of meat in our diet). Fish has always been easy and quick to cook but what has struck me, while working on this chapter, is how much more *convenient* it is to cook fish for one than for a whole family: the average grill or frying-pan can accommodate two fillets beautifully, but if you have to cook more than that it has to be done in relays, which means that some of it is always hanging about.

As with eggs (see previous chapter), I have tried to find ways to avoid expensively heating up an oven to cook one helping of fish, and I have been delighted by how successful the idea of 'foil-baking' it under the grill has been – that is, wrapping it in an individual parcel of foil to cook in its own juices. And, on a more personal level, there has been one more bonus. The very thought of peeling fresh prawns for four or six people has often made me think twice – but the joy of peeling prawns for one in less than 10 minutes is a different matter! Working on this book has reminded me how vastly superior their flavour is to the ready peeled frozen variety.

Plaice fillets gratinée

Actually any flat fish can be used for this recipe – sole, lemon sole, plaice fillets or even those small frozen plaice fillets. The recipe is a good example of how, so often, the simple things work best.

8 oz plaice fillets (225 g)
1 oz butter (25 g)
2 oz breadcrumbs (50 g)
1 oz freshly grated Parmesan or other cheese (25 g)
1 spring onion, finely chopped
1 dessertspoon fresh chopped parsley
grated rind and juice of half a lemon
a little extra butter
salt and freshly milled black pepper

Switch the grill on to preheat at its highest setting and line the grill pan with a sheet of foil. Next melt the butter in a small saucepan and while it's melting, use a pastry brush to paint a little of the melting butter over the foil.

Next lay the fish (flesh side uppermost) on the foil and season it with salt and pepper. When the butter is melted add the breadcrumbs, cheese, spring onion, parsley and lemon rind to it and stir to combine everything thoroughly. Then spread the breadcrumb mixture evenly over the fish.

Dot a little extra butter in flecks here and there over the top, then grill the fish for 5 minutes or until the breadcrumbs have turned a rich golden-brown and the fish is cooked. Serve with the juice of half a lemon squeezed over.

Foil-baked salmon with dill and cucumber sauce

I've always thought that salmon cooked in foil in its own juices is much better than poaching it. I have now experimented with cooking it in foil parcels under the grill – and I'm happy to say it works perfectly.

1 salmon steak weighing 6–8 oz (175–225 g)
½ oz butter (10 g)
1 pinch dried dill or ¼ teaspoon of fresh dill
1 slice of onion
1 bayleaf
2 tablespoons white wine or dry cider
salt and freshly milled black pepper

For the sauce:

1½ oz cucumber (40 g)
a small knob butter (approx ½ oz, 10 g)
⅛ teaspoon dried dill or ½ teaspoon fresh
1 level teaspoon flour
1 teaspoon lemon juice
1 dessertspoon cream
salt and freshly milled black pepper

Preheat the grill. And you'll also need a 12 inch (30 cm) square sheet of foil

I think it's best to cook this in a heatproof gratin dish. Using a piece of kitchen paper, smear a little of the butter over the centre of the foil before placing it on the gratin dish. Then place the salmon steak in the centre, season it lightly and sprinkle with dill, then place the slice of onion and a bayleaf in the cavity in the centre. Spoon the white wine (or cider) over, then seal the foil at the top, folding it over in a pleat three or four times, and do the same at each end, making a neat leak-proof package. Place the dish under the grill about 4 inches (10 cm) from the heat, and cook the salmon for 20 minutes.

Meanwhile start to make the sauce: melt the butter in a small saucepan and chop the piece of cucumber into small cubes (leaving the skin on).

Add these to the butter along with a little salt and pepper and the dill. Stir the cucumber around to get it all coated with butter, then put a lid on and let it cook gently in its own juice for about 6 minutes on the lowest possible heat – you might need to give it a stir once or twice.

After that sprinkle in the flour and stir to soak up the juices. When the salmon is cooked, carefully unwrap the foil and pour all the juices in the foil into a jug. Keep the fish warm while you gradually stir the fish liquid into the sauce. Finally, add the lemon juice and cream. Then carefully remove the skin from the fish, transfer it to a warm plate, pour the sauce over and serve.

Chilled salmon with tarragon sauce

For this you cook the salmon in exactly the same way as above, using 1/4 teaspoon of fresh chopped tarragon (1/4 teaspoon of dried) instead of the dill and omitting the wine. Open up the foil parcel to check that the fish is cooked, then re-seal it and leave the salmon to get quite cold.

When you're ready to serve, remove the skin and scrape off any congealed butter, and discard the onion and bayleaf. Serve garnished with water-cress and the tarragon sauce, *which is made quite simply by mixing together all the following ingredients:*

1 tablespoon mayonnaise (*see page 172*)
1 dessertspoon cream
1/2 teaspoon fresh chopped tarragon or 1/2 teaspoon dried tarragon soaked in 1 teaspoon of lemon juice for a few minutes before adding the whole lot
1/2 spring onion, finely chopped

Portuguese baked fish

I think this is best baked in the oven. However, if you prefer you can half cook the fish under the grill, pour on the sauce and finish cooking it the same way — in which case it should take no more than 15 minutes.

1 thick fillet of white fish (cod, hake, haddock, etc) weighing 6–8 oz (175–225 g)
1 small onion, finely chopped
½ small green pepper (2 oz, 50 g), chopped
1 clove of garlic, crushed
3 ripe tomatoes, peeled and chopped or 3 heaped dessertspoons of Italian chopped tomatoes
2 tablespoons white wine or dry cider
1 dessertspoon olive oil
1 tablespoon lemon juice
2 or 3 black olives, roughly chopped
salt and freshly milled black pepper

Preheat the oven to gas mark 5, 375°F, 190°C

Begin by making the sauce, which if you make it in a frying-pan will reduce and thicken very quickly. Heat the oil in the pan and in it fry the onion and pepper together for 6–8 minutes until they're softened and golden. Then add the garlic and after a minute or so pour in the tomatoes and the white wine (or cider). Season, give it a good stir, then simmer the sauce gently for about 10 minutes until it has reduced and become quite thick.

Next, place the fish in a gratin dish, season with salt and pepper, and sprinkle with the lemon juice. Cover it with the sauce, sprinkle the chopped olives on top, then cover the dish loosely with a piece of foil. Bake on a high shelf in the oven for 20 minutes. Then remove the foil and give it another five minutes. This just needs some boiled new potatoes (if the season is right).

Right: Quick French onion soup, page 28; Cheese soufflé omelette with spinach filling, page 45.

Goujons of lemon sole with herbs

These are little strips of fish coated in egg and breadcrumbs then deep-fried – the addition of a few herbs to the coating does make them more special. When you buy the fish, ask your fishmonger to skin the fillets for you, because it's fiddly to do them yourself (and it needs a really sharp knife).

1 large or 2 small fillets of lemon sole, skinned (you need 5 oz, 150 g, or so altogether)
1 tablespoon seasoned flour
1 small egg, beaten
5 tablespoons fresh breadcrumbs
1 teaspoon chopped fresh thyme or ½ teaspoon dried
½ teaspoon bruised, chopped rosemary
1 tablespoon fresh chopped parsley
1 small clove of garlic, finely chopped
oil for deep-frying
salt and freshly milled black pepper

First of all pat the fish dry with kitchen paper, then cut the fillets into thinnish (½–¾ inch, 1–2 cm) strips diagonally against the grain. Now spread the seasoned flour out on a large flat plate, and have the beaten egg ready in a bowl. Mix the breadcrumbs together with the chopped herbs and garlic, spread this mixture out on a large plate, and have that ready to hand as well.

Now roll the strips of fish in the flour, then dip them in the beaten egg, and finally roll them under the palm of your hand in the breadcrumb-and-herb mixture to get them well and truly coated.

Next heat the oil in a deep pan up to 350°F, 180°C. If you don't have a thermometer, drop a cube of bread in and if it turns crisp and golden in 1 minute, the oil is hot enough. Deep-fry the goujons for 2 minutes until golden brown, then drain them on crumpled greaseproof paper (you may need to do these in two batches). Sprinkle with salt and pepper and serve with homemade tartare sauce (*see page 173*).

Left: Provençale crusted cod, page 69; Mozzarella in carrozza, page 192.

Cheese-crusted fish pie

This is amazingly quick to make – thirty minutes at the very most. Instead of all the bother of cooking mashed potatoes, you simply part-cook them, grate them and mix with the cheese.

6 oz white fish fillet, any variety (175 g)
2 medium potatoes, not more than 6 oz, 175 g, altogether
1 egg
1 bayleaf
a few parsley stalks
7 fl oz milk (200 ml)
½ oz butter (10 g)
1 rounded dessertspoon flour (½ oz, 10 g)
1 dessertspoon lemon juice
1 teaspoon capers
1 small gherkin, chopped
1 tablespoon fresh chopped parsley
1 oz Cheddar cheese (25 g), grated
a little extra butter
salt and freshly milled black pepper

You also need an oval gratin dish, buttered

Scrub the potatoes, but don't peel them, then put them in a saucepan together with the egg. (I know this is a little unorthodox, but it saves heat and washing-up!) Add some salt, then pour boiling water over and boil the potatoes for 15 minutes – but take the egg out after 10.

While that's happening, place the fish in another pan together with the bayleaf and a few parsley stalks, season and pour in the milk. Bring it up to simmering point and simmer for 5–6 minutes, or until the fish is cooked. Then strain the cooking milk into a jug and transfer the fish to a plate to keep warm.

Now wipe the pan over, then add the butter to it and melt it over a medium heat. Stir in the flour till smooth, then pour in the reserved milk, stirring after each addition till you have a smooth sauce. Season and let it cook gently for 3 minutes. Then when the potatoes are ready, drain them and leave them to cool until they can be handled.

Now remove the skin from the fish and flake it; peel the egg and chop it up roughly. Add these to the sauce together with the chopped parsley, lemon juice, capers and gherkin. Taste the seasoning at this stage, then preheat the grill. Next (using a cloth to hold them if they are still a bit hot) peel the potatoes and then grate them on the coarse side of the grater into a bowl. Mix carefully with the grated cheese.

Pour the fish mixture into the gratin dish, smoothing it out, and top it with the cheese-and-potato mixture, spreading it out as evenly as possible. Dot the surface of the potato with a few flecks of butter and grill (4 inches (10 cm) from the heat) for 10–12 minutes or until brown and crusty.

Fried herrings in oatmeal and crushed pepper

Herrings can be the nicest fish of all – when they're fresh. So look out for bright eyes and scales like polished silver on them, then you know they're fresh.

2 smallish fresh herrings, gutted
1½ tablespoons medium oatmeal
¾ teaspoon black peppercorns, coarsely crushed
1½ tablespoons olive oil
salt

Serve with: lemon wedges

To prepare the herrings, use a sharp knife to cut off the heads and tails. Then take a pair of scissors and cut them open all along their bellies. Now turn them skin-side up on a flat surface and flatten them out, giving them quite sharp bashes with your fist: press hard with your thumbs along the backbone to loosen it, then turn the fish over and lift the backbone at the head end and carefully peel it away from the flesh so that it takes all the small bones with it.

Now heat the oil in a heavy-based 7 inch (18 cm) frying-pan, and while it's heating wipe the herrings over with kitchen paper to get them quite dry. Sprinkle the oatmeal on a plate, then coat the herrings with this on both sides (pressing it well in). Next sprinkle the flesh side of the fish with the crushed pepper (pressing that well in too). Fry the fish in the hot oil, skin-side down first, for 4 minutes then turn them over and fry on the other side for 4 minutes. Drain them on absorbent kitchen paper or crumpled greaseproof paper, season with salt and serve with some lemon squeezed over.

Foil-baked fish with lemon sauce

If switching on the oven for one solitary piece of cod seems extravagant – fear not. You can 'foil-bake' your fish under the grill, and it's even quicker.

8 oz fish steak (225 g)
1 dessertspoon lemon juice
½ oz butter (10 g)
1 dessertspoon fresh chopped parsley
1 dessertspoon chopped celery leaves
a little extra butter
salt and freshly milled black pepper

For the sauce:

1 slice of lemon
3 fl oz water (75 ml)
½ oz butter (10 g)
1 level dessertspoon flour
1 dessertspoon lemon juice

First preheat the grill to its highest setting. Then take a piece of foil large enough to wrap the fish in, and butter it (to prevent the fish sticking). You can do this by placing a knob of butter in the centre and smearing it out using kitchen paper.

Now place the fish on the foil, sprinkle the lemon juice over, then spread the ½ oz (10 g) of butter over the top. Season with salt and pepper and sprinkle over the parsley and celery leaves, pressing them into the butter. Now bring the sides of the foil up to the centre, make a pleat in the top, then keep folding it down until you reach the fish and have a seam. Then crimp and fold the ends of the foil over so that you have a neat, well sealed parcel.

Place the fish parcel under the grill and after 6 minutes turn it over and let it cook on the other side for 6 minutes.

Meanwhile you can be making the sauce: first boil the slice of lemon in the water (with a lid on the pan) for 5 minutes, and then strain it into a jug and discard the lemon. Now in the same saucepan melt the butter and stir in the flour, and when it's absolutely smooth gradually add the lemon water, stirring well after each addition until you have a smooth sauce. Now add the other dessertspoon of lemon juice and simmer gently for about 3 minutes.

When the fish is ready, carefully open the parcel and pour out all the buttery juices into the sauce, and taste and season with salt and pepper. Finally return the fish with the foil opened out to the grill for a further 2 minutes or so to finish cooking. Serve the fish with the sauce poured over – and all it needs with it is plain boiled potatoes.

Provençale crusted cod with Provençale tomatoes

This is virtually an all-in-one meal cooked under the grill, except perhaps it needs a few new potatoes and a green salad to accompany it.

1 piece of cod or fresh haddock weighing 6–8 oz (175–225 g)
2 medium ripe red tomatoes
2 tablespoons breadcrumbs
1 level tablespoon fresh chopped herbs (a mixture of parsley, thyme and tarragon – or if these are not available use ½ teaspoon dried thyme, ½ teaspoon dried tarragon and 1 tablespoon parsley)
1 clove of garlic, crushed
grated zest of half a lemon
juice of half a lemon
2 tablespoons olive oil
a little extra oil
salt and freshly milled black pepper

First of all preheat the grill, then in a basin simply mix the breadcrumbs, herbs, garlic and lemon zest with half the lemon juice and the 2 tablespoons of olive oil till thoroughly blended. Then season well with salt and freshly milled pepper.

Next oil a small baking-sheet or fireproof gratin dish, then place the fish on this along with the tomatoes cut into halves. Now spread two-thirds of the breadcrumb mixture over the fish, pressing it firmly into the flesh. Spoon the rest over the tomato halves. Sprinkle a few more drops of olive oil over everything, then place the whole lot under the grill – at the position furthest away from the heat – and grill for 10–15 minutes or until the fish is cooked and the crust is crisp.

Serve straightaway with the rest of the lemon juice sprinkled over the fish.

Poached fish with gherkin and caper sauce

Finely chopped watercress goes well in this sauce but if you have none to hand, parsley will make a good substitute.

1 piece of white fish (cod, haddock, whiting, etc) weighing approx 8 oz (225 g)
2 fl oz dry white wine or dry cider (55 ml)
¾ teaspoon dried or fresh tarragon
1 bayleaf
¾ oz butter (20 g)
1 level teaspoon flour
1 tablespoon natural yoghurt
2 gherkins, finely chopped
1 teaspoon of capers, drained
1 spring onion, finely chopped
1 tablespoon finely chopped watercress leaves
salt and freshly milled black pepper

Begin by pouring the wine onto the dried tarragon, so that it can soak for a minute or two. Then put the fish in a small saucepan, add the bayleaf, then pour the wine (plus tarragon) over and add some salt and pepper.

Bring the fish up to simmering point and barely simmer it for about 5–10 minutes depending on its thickness. Meanwhile melt the butter in a separate saucepan and stir in the flour till smooth. When the fish is cooked, strain off the liquid into a jug and keep the fish warm.

Gradually add the fish-cooking liquid to the flour-and-butter mixture, stirring all the time until you have a smooth glossy sauce, then simmer for a minute or so. Now, off the heat, add the yoghurt, gherkins, capers, spring onion and watercress and stir till smooth. Taste and season with salt and pepper, then reheat very gently. Serve the fish with the sauce poured over. This is good served with creamed potatoes.

Kedgeree with kippers

I admit that, having tried kedgeree on several occasions with brown rice, I have now come to the conclusion that it is always better made with white rice (which also happens to be a lot quicker).

1 medium-sized kipper (or 4 oz, 110 g, kipper fillets)
5 fl oz liquid (see recipe) (150 ml)
1 oz butter (25 g)
½ medium onion (2 oz, 50 g), chopped
⅛ teaspoon Madras curry powder
⅓ teacup long-grain rice (up to the 2½ fl oz, 60 ml level in a glass measuring jug)
1 dessertspoon lemon juice
3 oz mushrooms (75 g), sliced
1 large egg, hardboiled
1 tablespoon fresh chopped parsley
cayenne pepper
salt and freshly milled black pepper

Lay the kipper in a shallow dish and pour a generous ½ pint (275 ml) of boiling water over to cover it, then leave on one side for 5 minutes: after that drain (reserving the water) and flake the fish, discarding the skin, head and bones.

Now strain 5 fl oz (150 ml) of the reserved water into a jug and keep it on one side. Next heat half the butter in a saucepan and fry the onion for 5 minutes to soften before stirring in the curry powder and the rice. Cook for 1 minute then add the reserved strained stock. Bring to simmering point, cover and cook over a low heat until the rice has absorbed the liquid and is tender – about 15 minutes.

Next melt the rest of the butter in a separate pan, add the lemon juice and cook the mushrooms till tender (about 3 minutes). Then add the contents of the pan to the cooked rice together with the flaked fish. Peel and chop the hardboiled egg and add that to the rice as well, then fork everything in carefully, trying not to break up the fish. Taste and season with salt and pepper as required.

Serve in a warmed dish, garnished with parsley and an extra knob of butter. (I like to serve this with a sprinkling of cayenne, too.)

Prawns in chilli sauce

The best choice for this, if you can get one, is a fresh chilli deseeded and chopped; but failing that ½ level teaspoon of chilli powder would do. If you put some brown rice on to cook before you start this, the two should be ready almost simultaneously.

3–4 oz frozen peeled prawns (75–110 g), defrosted
6 oz red ripe tomatoes (175 g) or a 7 oz can of Italian tomatoes (200 g)
1 small onion, chopped small
1 oz green pepper (25 g), chopped
1 tablespoon oil
1 clove of garlic, crushed
3 olives (preferably black), stoned and chopped
chilli (see above)
1 dessertspoon lemon juice
salt and freshly milled black pepper

First, if you're using fresh tomatoes, pour boiling water over them and then after a few minutes just slip the skins off, then chop the flesh roughly.

Now heat one tablespoon of oil in a medium-sized saucepan, add the onion and soften it for 5 minutes before adding the chopped pepper and garlic. Cook these for a further 5 minutes, then stir in the prepared tomatoes, the olives, chilli and a seasoning of salt and pepper. Carry on cooking – at a gentle simmer – for about 20 minutes (uncovered) till the excess liquid has evaporated and the mixture has thickened up a bit.

After that add the prawns and let them heat through for a further 5 minutes. Taste to check the seasoning, and the chilli strength, then add the lemon juice and serve on a bed of rice.

Salmon and caper fish cakes

I've adapted this from a Jewish recipe in which the cakes are coated in matzo meal before frying. Failing that of course wholewheat or even plain flour will do perfectly well. If you can plan ahead you can arrange to make enough mashed potato at a previous meal to cover this one as well.

3½ oz tin of red salmon
approx 4 oz mashed potato (110 g)
¼ teaspoon dried dill
1 dessertspoon lemon juice
cayenne pepper
freshly grated nutmeg
1 egg, hardboiled, chopped small
1 dessertspoon capers, drained and chopped a bit
1 heaped tablespoon chopped parsley
flour (see above), seasoned with salt and pepper
2 tablespoons groundnut oil
salt and freshly milled black pepper

For the garnish: watercress and lemon segments

Begin by stirring the dill into the lemon juice to soak for 5 minutes. Meanwhile drain off the oil from the salmon and take off any skin and bone. Then, in a mixing bowl, mash it down with a fork, season with salt and pepper, and add the lemon juice (plus dill), a good pinch of cayenne and a grating of nutmeg.

Next add the mashed potato, chopped hardboiled eggs, capers and parsley and carry on mixing with the fork until everything is thoroughly blended. Now taste to check the seasoning. Next take about one-third of the mixture and shape it into a round cake (using your hands); do the same with the rest of the mixture, then coat each fish cake with the seasoned wholewheat flour.

Heat the oil in a frying-pan, then shallow-fry the cakes for a few minutes on each side till they're a nice golden colour, drain on kitchen paper, and serve garnished with sprigs of watercress and segments of lemon to squeeze over. (I like to serve these with rice cooked with onion then garnished with chopped parsley and flavoured with lemon juice – yummy!)

Chilled marinated trout with pepper and tomatoes

This is a very quick and easy recipe. Because it benefits from a few hours' marinating, it can be made ahead of time for when you're going to be late home. On the other hand, if you're no good at planning ahead, it's equally delicious served hot (with new potatoes and a green salad).

1 trout weighing 8–10 oz (225–275 g) – or you can buy two small ones if you've got a big appetite

4 oz ripe red tomatoes (110 g)

½ small green pepper, finely chopped

½ smallish onion, chopped small

½ teaspoon dried oregano

3 thin slices of lemon

2 fl oz dry white wine or dry cider (55 ml)

1 tablespoon olive oil

1 tablespoon wine vinegar

1 level teaspoon capers

salt and freshly milled black pepper

For the garnish: fresh chopped parsley

First pour hot water over the tomatoes, and after a couple of minutes slip the skins off and chop up the flesh. Then in a 7 inch (18 cm) frying-pan place all the ingredients (except the trout), season with salt and pepper, then bring the mixture up to simmering point, cover the pan with a large plate and simmer gently for 20 minutes.

After that, using a tea-cloth or gloves to protect your hands, lift the plate off and add the trout to the pan. Taste to check the seasoning, then let the trout simmer in the sauce for about 7 minutes – turning it over halfway through.

Then remove the trout to a shallow oval dish, pour all the sauce over it, and when it's quite cold cover the dish with clingfilm and chill in the fridge until you want it. This goes well with a rice salad and fresh bread.

Kashmir spiced prawns

This is a fresh, mildly spicy curry – and very quick to make. If you would like it a bit more fiery, I suggest you add ¼ teaspoon of chilli powder. Another point: if you don't want to grind your spices, you can use instead 1 level teaspoon hot curry powder, ½ teaspoon turmeric and ½ teaspoon powdered ginger.

4 oz prawns (110 g), peeled weight
1 dessertspoon groundnut oil
1 medium onion, chopped
¼ green pepper, chopped
1 clove of garlic, crushed
½ lb red ripe tomatoes (225 g), skinned and chopped *or* **a 7 oz tin of Italian tomatoes (200 g)**
2 inches cucumber (5 cm), peeled and chopped
1 teaspoon mango chutney juice
1 tablespoon natural yoghurt

For the spices:

¼ teaspoon cumin seeds
¼ teaspoon coriander seeds
½ teaspoon turmeric
1 cardamom pod
⅛ teaspoon chilli powder
1 inch fresh ginger (2·5 cm), grated

If you're using the fresh spices, start off by grinding them finely using a pestle and mortar. Then in a medium-sized saucepan heat the oil and fry the onion, pepper and garlic in it for 5 minutes. Next add the spices, stirring them around to allow the heat to draw out their flavour and aroma.

After about 5 minutes stir in the chopped tomatoes and cucumber, stir thoroughly and let the whole thing simmer gently (without a lid) for about 6 minutes before adding the prawns, chutney juice and yoghurt. Allow these to heat through gently for another 5 minutes without it boiling, then serve with spiced or plain Basmati rice.

Gratinée of prawns with avocado

Don't be put off this by having to peel the prawns yourself. Fresh ones are larger and juicier and have more flavour than the frozen, ready-shelled kind. I timed this little lot myself and it only took ten minutes, and with Top of the Pops *on the TV I hardly noticed it!*

½ lb large prawns in their shells (225 g)
½ ripe avocado pear (the other half can be wrapped in clingfilm, stored in the refrigerator and eaten next day with the vinaigrette dressing on *p. 171*)
2½ fl oz brown or white rice (60 ml), cooked according to the method on *page 134*
1 oz butter (25 g)
¾ oz flour (20 g)
¼ pint dry white wine or dry cider (150 ml)
prawn stock (see recipe)
2 tablespoons cream
juice of half a lemon
1 oz grated Gruyère or other cheese (25 g)
1 tablespoon wholemeal breadcrumbs
pinch of cayenne
salt and freshly milled black pepper

First cook the rice and keep it warm with a clean tea-towel over the pan. Now peel the prawns (scraping out any of the black threads that run down the back) and put them to one side. Then place the shells and debris in a sieve and rinse under the cold tap. Now place the lot in a saucepan with cold water to just cover: add a little salt, bring up to the boil and simmer for 15 minutes.

Meanwhile melt the butter in another saucepan and stir in the flour till smooth, then gradually stir in the wine, a little at a time, until you have a smooth glossy paste. Next strain the prawn shells (discarding them) and measure ¼ pint (150 ml) of the prawn stock into a jug. Finish off the sauce by stirring this in a little at a time, simmer gently for 10 minutes, stirring in the cream at the end.

While that's happening, preheat the grill. Remove the skin from the half avocado, slice the flesh in half lengthways and then across so that you have bite-sized chunks.

Now spread the rice over the base of a buttered 7 inch (18 cm) or 9 inch (23 cm) gratin dish, then spread the chunks of avocado in a layer followed by the prawns. Season these with a little salt and pepper and sprinkle the lemon juice over. Now pour the sauce over, sprinkle the cheese and breadcrumbs over the surface and finish with a pinch of cayenne. Grill at the position furthest away from the grill for about 10 minutes, by which time the prawns and avocado will be heated through and the sauce brown and bubbling.

Grilled trout with garlic, lemon and caper sauce

This one is lightning quick!

1 trout weighing 8–10 oz (225–275 g)
1 dessertspoon olive oil
½ smallish onion, finely chopped
1 clove garlic, chopped
1 oz butter or alternative (25 g)
1 level teaspoon flour
3 fl oz dry white wine or dry cider (75 ml)
1 oz capers (25 g), drained
1 dessertspoon lemon juice
1 teaspoon grated lemon zest
1 tablespoon fresh chopped parsley
salt and freshly milled black pepper

First rinse and dry the trout thoroughly with a clean cloth or kitchen paper. Preheat the grill, and while that's happening line the grill pan with foil and paint the foil quite liberally with olive oil.

Then place the fish on the foil and paint the top of that, too, with olive oil and season with salt and freshly milled pepper. Next grill the fish for about 3–4 minutes, then turn it over, baste with the juices and grill the other side for 3–4 minutes. (Incidentally, while that's going on you can be warming a plate underneath the grill pan.)

Meanwhile, in a small saucepan soften the onion and garlic in the butter for 5 minutes, then stir in the flour to soak up all the juice and gradually add the wine, a little at a time, stirring all the while to make a smooth sauce. Next add the capers, lemon juice, and zest, and simmer the sauce gently (without a lid) for 5–6 minutes.

When the trout is cooked, transfer it carefully to a plate using a fish slice. Pour any juice in the foil into the sauce, stir in the parsley, then pour over the fish. Serve with plain new potatoes.

Plaice fillets tartare

These are plaice fillets cooked with *tartare sauce as a coating, and I really do recommend you use homemade tartare sauce for this if possible* (see page 173). *The result, I can promise, is well worth it.*

2 fillets of plaice
2 well-heaped teaspoons tartare sauce
1 oz butter (25 g)
2 tablespoons grated Cheddar cheese
1 tablespoon breadcrumbs
1 tablespoon chopped parsley
1 pinch of cayenne
salt and freshly milled black pepper

Preheat the grill, first of all. Then line the grill pan, or else a heatproof dish that will accommodate both fillets side by side, with a sheet of foil and butter it by rubbing a little of the butter over it with kitchen paper. Now place the fillets skin-side down on the foil, season them with salt and pepper, then dot each one with flecks of butter. Grill the fish, approximately 3 inches (7·5 cm) from the heat for 7 minutes, basting occasionally with the buttery juices.

While that's happening mix the grated cheese together with the breadcrumbs, parsley and a pinch of cayenne together in a bowl. Then when the fish is ready, spread each fillet with a generously heaped teaspoon of tartare sauce, making sure all the top surface is covered. Next sprinkle the cheese-and-breadcrumb mixture over them, and return them to underneath the grill to cook for a further 3 minutes until the cheese is golden-brown and bubbling. Serve them straightaway.

Crab and mushrooms au gratin

You can buy dressed crab-meat packed into the shell – a small one will yield you 3 oz (75 g) of meat (brown and white) which is just about right for this.

long-grain rice measured to the 2 fl oz level in a glass measuring jug (55 ml)
4 fl oz water (110 g)
3 oz crabmeat (75 g)
1 small onion, chopped small
2 oz mushrooms (50 g), sliced
1 oz butter (25 g)
½ oz flour (10 g)
1 tablespoon dry sherry
5 fl oz milk (150 ml)
1 tablespoon grated Cheddar cheese
1 tablespoon breadcrumbs
cayenne pepper
salt and freshly milled black pepper

For this you will need a 7 inch (18 cm) or 9 inch (23 cm) oval gratin dish. Start off by cooking the rice in the water (with a little salt added) until all the water has been absorbed and the rice is tender. Then fluff it up with a fork and arrange it over the base of the gratin dish.

While the rice is cooking, preheat the grill and melt the butter in a small heavy-based saucepan. Add the onion and cook gently for 5 minutes to soften before adding the sliced mushrooms. Stir them around to get them nicely coated, then cook for a further 5 minutes over a fairly gentle heat. After that stir in the flour, cook for another minute then add the sherry. Stir this in, then gradually add the milk – stirring – until you have a smooth sauce. Season with salt and pepper and cook gently for another 5 minutes.

Next spread the crabmeat evenly over the rice, then when it's ready pour the mushroom and onion sauce over the crab. Mix the grated cheese and breadcrumbs together with a pinch or two of cayenne, then sprinkle this over the top. Grill for 5 minutes until golden and bubbling, then serve at once.

One Man's Meat...

Boboutie

New England chilli bowl

Fillet steak with mustard and juniper sauce

Pan-fried toad-in-the-hole

Bangers and mash with browned onion and mustard sauce

Cheese and herb crusted cottage pie

Individual steak, kidney and mushroom pie

Steak and kidney with puréed vegetable topping

Braised steak au poivre

Beef curry cooked in yoghurt

Oriental lamb

Baked lamb with potato, garlic and rosemary

Piquant liver with sherry sauce

Lamb chops baked with aubergines

Kofta kebab

Cider-braised pork with cream and mushrooms

Porc au poivre

Barbecued pork slices

Stuffed pork chop with fennel

Hung shao pork

Baked Hungarian pork chop

Chicken chasseur

Poached breast of chicken with cream and mushrooms

Chicken tikka kebab

Chicken in paprika sauce

Gammon steak with honey and mustard sauce

Chinese stir-fried chicken with broccoli and mushrooms

Pork chop with apples and cider

Gammon steak with gherkin sauce

Fried chicken breast with cheese

Chicken breast with preserved ginger sauce

Chicken Véronique

Poulet Basque

One is fun!

The pay-off to this familiar phrase (. . . another man's poison) is currently the subject of a great deal of public discussion. The debate has sometimes engendered fears that have sent lots of people flocking like sheep – no pun intended – to the greener pastures of vegetarianism. I don't intend to pursue the discussion here, except to say that the word that so often gets left out is 'less'.

A drastic about-turn is not necessarily the answer. If a person's diet contains a lot of animal fat from other sources (pastries, pies, chocolates) then clearly some sort of restraint is called for. Equally, for someone who doesn't indulge between meals and who eats a normally well-balanced diet, eating a piece of meat three or four times a week scarcely puts them into the living-dangerously bracket! Last year some animal rights campaigners put the fear of God into the nation by claiming (falsely as it turned out) to have poisoned some Mars Bars. The most enlightening thing to emerge from this episode, though, was the news that this country consumes three million Mars Bars a day!

Exactly. A realistic assessment of the fat-content of the nation's diet would include a survey of the number of sweet-wrappers, pie-cartons, etc left after a journey on any inter-city train, as well as a judgment on the number of pork chops we consume. My message is, as it always has been, moderation: meat as a main course on three days a week, eggs on one, fish on one other and some form of vegetarian meal on the rest constitute a perfectly acceptable, interesting and varied diet.

So no apologies for the recipes in this chapter, but just one point to make about them. I have quite deliberately concentrated here on the quicker-cooking cuts of meat, because many of the others require long slow cooking in the oven. The cost of gas or electricity being what it is, the economic equation simply does not work out in their favour for one person. Where I *have* included cuts that call for long cooking, they are normally slow-simmered on top of the stove.

Boboutie

This just goes to show you can make something really special with ordinary minced beef. The recipe comes from Africa, but seems to me to have an interesting mixture of European and oriental overtones.

4 oz minced beef (110 g)
1 small onion, chopped
½ small cooking apple (approx 2 oz, 50 g), chopped (you can use the rest of the apple in a salad)
½ oz butter (10 g)
10 whole almonds, roughly chopped
½ level teaspoon hot curry powder
½ teaspoon brown sugar
1 dessertspoon lemon juice
1 large egg
2½ fl oz milk (60 ml)
½ oz bread without crusts (brown or white) (10 g)
salt and freshly milled black pepper

Preheat the oven to gas mark 2, 300°F, 150°C

Start off by heating the butter in a heavy-based frying-pan, then add the onion and apple and cook gently for 10 minutes to soften. After that stir in the chopped almonds, turn the heat up and add the minced beef. Cook for 5 minutes or so, stirring the meat around the pan to colour it evenly, then add the curry powder, sugar, lemon juice and a seasoning of salt and pepper.

Leave the mixture to cook for a few minutes more. Meanwhile add the egg to the milk in a basin and whisk them together well. Now pour half of the egg-and-milk mixture onto the bread and let it soak for 5 minutes, and when it's soft beat it well and add to the meat mixture.

Transfer the whole lot to a 1 pint (570 ml) ovenproof dish, pour the rest of the egg-and-milk mixture over the top and bake in the oven for 45 minutes.

New England chilli bowl

I've suggested two ways of cooking this delicious, spicy main meal: you can either cook it the traditional way in a slow oven, or (if you want to cut down on gas or electricity) it can be done on top of the stove by using a little more liquid.

2 oz red kidney beans (50 g)
4 oz good quality minced beef (110 g)
oil
1 small onion, chopped
1 small clove of garlic, crushed
½ teaspoon cumin seeds
¼ teaspoon crushed dried chilli or chilli powder
1 dessertspoon flour
1 tablespoon tomato purée
6 fl oz hot water (175 ml), if cooking on top of the stove (5 fl oz, 150 ml, if cooking in the oven)
½ small red or green pepper, sliced
salt and freshly milled black pepper

Start by placing the kidney beans in a saucepan, covering them with plenty of cold water, bringing it up to the boil then turning off the heat and leaving the beans to soak. It's best to start this off before you go to work in the morning or if you work at home they need soaking for at least 2 hours.

When you're ready to cook, bring the beans back to the boil, boil briskly for 10 minutes and then drain them. Meanwhile heat 1½ tablespoons of oil in a medium-sized pan or small flameproof casserole, add the onion and garlic and cook for 5 minutes to soften before turning up the heat and adding the minced beef. Cook this, stirring it round the pan, to colour evenly.

Next crush the cumin seeds and add them to the pan together with the chilli powder. Cook for a minute or so then sprinkle in the flour, stirring it in to soak up the juices. Now stir the tomato purée into the required quantity of hot water (see above), then gradually add this to the pan, stirring after each addition. When it's all in, add the drained beans, bring up to the boil and cover the pan or casserole.

Now either place it in the centre of the oven (preheated to gas mark 2,

300°F, 150°C) or else set it on top of the stove to cook at a *gentle* simmer. Cook for 1 hour (giving it the occasional stir, if on top of the stove) then after that season with salt and pepper and stir in the sliced pepper. Cook for a further half an hour or until the beans are quite tender. Serve with plain rice or creamed potato.

Fillet steak with mustard and juniper sauce

This is definitely for feast days, as it is really rather extravagant, but it can also be made with pork fillet, but that would need 10–15 minutes' initial cooking.

6–8 oz fillet steak (175–225 g)
½ teaspoon juniper berries
⅓ teaspoon black peppercorns
1 small onion
½ oz butter (10 g)
1 teaspoon oil
2 oz mushrooms (50 g), sliced
1 rounded teaspoon mustard powder
1 teaspoon lemon juice
3 fl oz white wine or dry cider (75 ml)
1 tablespoon cream
salt

First of all crush the juniper berries and peppercorns in a pestle and mortar (or else use the back of a tablespoon on a flat surface). Then cut the steak into round slices and the slices into ¼ inch (5 mm) strips about 1½–2 inches (4–5 cm) long. Peel and slice the onion, then cut the slices in half and separate them out into half-moon shapes.

Now heat the butter and oil in a heavy-based 7 inch (18 cm) frying-pan and fry the onion over a medium heat for 5 minutes to soften before adding the mushrooms and cooking for a further 5 minutes. After that push them over to one side of the pan, turn the heat up, and add the pieces of steak. Sprinkle in the crushed peppercorns and juniper, then almost immediately turn the heat down again to medium and cook the steak briefly (4–5 minutes in all, depending on how you like your steak).

Meanwhile mix the mustard with the lemon juice and wine, then pour the mixture over the steak. Let it bubble and reduce for about one minute. Stir the mushrooms and onion into the sauce, then stir in the cream. Taste to check the seasoning, and serve with plain boiled rice and a salad.

Pan-fried toad-in-the-hole

I was unable to make an authentic Yorkshire pudding batter for this (as one egg makes enough for four servings!). But I did make a very successful unauthentic batter – very light and crisp and delightfully easy.

5 or 6 good quality chipolata sausages (or more or less according to how hungry you are)
1 small egg
1 dessertspoon oil
1 small onion, sliced into rings
1 oz plain flour (25 g)
2 tablespoons milk
½ teaspoon mixed herbs
salt and freshly milled black pepper

Heat the oil, first of all, in a heavy 7 inch (18 cm) frying-pan then over a medium heat fry the chipolatas and onion rings together for about 10 minutes. Meanwhile preheat the grill and make up the batter.

To do this you sieve the flour into a bowl, make a well in the centre and break the egg into it. Now whisk the egg, gradually incorporating the flour and finally whisk in the milk, until you have a smooth, lump-free batter (you may need to stir round the edge of the bowl and have another whisk to make sure it's all blended). Then season with salt and pepper, and whisk in the herbs.

By this time the chipolatas will be ready, so increase the heat to its highest setting, and when it is very hot pour in the batter all round the chipolatas. Then leave it, without stirring or anything, for 1 or 2 minutes or until it looks on the point of bubbling up slightly here and there.

It will look a total disaster at this stage, but all is well. Just transfer the pan to sit under the grill (allowing room for the batter to rise) and let it finish cooking for about 6–10 minutes, or until it has become beautifully puffy and very crisp and brown. Now serve it immediately – it will shrink somewhat but remain light and crisp.

Bangers and mash with browned onion and mustard sauce

The lovely caramelised flavour of the onions in the sauce really does lift this out of the everyday level.

6–8 oz good quality pork sausages (175–225 g)
mashed potato (see recipe)
4 fl oz potato stock, reserved from cooking the potatoes (110 ml)
1 dessertspoon oil
1 medium onion, thinly sliced
½ teaspoon granulated sugar
½ teaspoon flour
1 heaped teaspoon mustard powder
10 whole peppercorns, coarsely crushed
4 fl oz dry white wine or dry cider (110 ml)
salt

Grill or fry the sausages, and cook your required quantity of potatoes then mash them. (If you are using a heavy-gauge aluminium pan you can whisk them in the pan with a knob of butter and some milk, using an electric hand-whisk, which will make them light and fluffy; for variations on the theme you could add a tablespoon of cottage cheese, or yoghurt, or cream or even an ounce of cream cheese with herbs.) Reserve the water in which the potatoes were cooked.

Now for the sauce. While the sausages and potatoes are cooking, heat the oil in a frying-pan and when it's very hot add the onion and sprinkle in the sugar (which will help to caramelise them) – they need about 10–15 minutes with the heat at medium and you'll have to stir them around the pan quite often.

When they have reached the toasted dark-brown stage, sprinkle in the flour, mustard and crushed peppercorns and stir them in. Now gradually add the reserved potato stock, followed by the white wine, stirring after each addition till you have a smooth sauce. Let it simmer for a minute or two then taste, season and serve.

Cheese and herb crusted cottage pie

This recipe is part of a Mixed Double. I believe it is worth going to the trouble of making twice as much mince filling as you need for this cottage pie (actually it's no more trouble than making a smaller quantity). You can then store half the mince mixture and use it next day in the recipe for spaghetti with Mexican sauce on page 126.

For the double mince mixture:

12 oz lean minced beef (350 g)
1 largish onion, roughly chopped
1 medium carrot, finely chopped
1 tablespoon oil
1 teaspoon mixed herbs, fresh or dried
1 level tablespoon flour
½ pint water (275 ml), mixed with 1 dessertspoon mushroom ketchup and 1 teaspoon Worcestershire sauce
salt and freshly milled black pepper

Heat the oil in a medium-sized saucepan then add the onion and carrot and cook them together for about 8 minutes until they have softened and browned slightly at the edges. Then, using a draining spoon, remove them to a plate. Now turn the heat up to high and brown the meat quickly in the pan, stirring it around until it too becomes brown and toasted at the edges.

Drain off the fat that has come out of it, then sprinkle in the mixed herbs and a seasoning of salt and pepper and return the carrot and onion to the pan. Next stir in the flour and then gradually add the water (with mushroom ketchup and Worcestershire sauce), stirring as you do so. Turn the heat down to the gentlest possible simmer, cover the pan, and simmer for 30 minutes.

When it's cooked, divide the mince in half, leave one half-quantity to get cold in a bowl, then cover the bowl and store this in the fridge for use the next day. The rest of the mince is now ready for the cottage pie.

For the cottage-pie topping:
6–7 oz potatoes (175–200 g)
1 tablespoon yoghurt
a knob of butter
1½ oz Double Gloucester cheese with Onion and Chives (40 g), grated
½ teaspoon mixed herbs, fresh or dried
salt

While the meat is simmering, cut the potatoes into chunks and boil them in salted water until tender, then drain them and return them to the pan. Add the yoghurt and butter, then mash them to a smooth purée. Then preheat the grill.

When the meat is cooked, taste to check the seasoning, and transfer one half-quantity to a 5 inch (13 cm) ramekin or small pie-dish. Then spoon the mashed potato mixture all over the top, levelling it off with a fork. Now combine the grated cheese with the herbs, and sprinkle this mixture all over the surface of the potato. Place the dish under the grill till the cheese is brown and bubbling.

Individual steak, kidney and mushroom pie

This is another of my Mixed Double recipes – the point being that if you are going to the trouble of cooking some steak and kidney, why not cook a double quantity, put half of it on one side in the fridge and have the steak and kidney with puréed vegetable topping (page 92) the following night? If you prefer not to do that simply halve the quantities below and make just one of the recipes.

For the double steak and kidney mixture:
12 oz steak and kidney (350 g) (i.e. 8 oz, 225 g, braising steak and 4 oz, 110 g, ox kidney) cut into small cubes
1 medium onion, chopped
1 tablespoon beef dripping or oil
½ teaspoon mixed herbs
1 tablespoon flour
½ pint hot water (275 ml), mixed with 1 dessertspoon mushroom ketchup and 1 teaspoon Worcestershire sauce
4 oz dark-gilled mushrooms (110 g), quartered
salt and freshly milled black pepper

In a small flameproof casserole heat the fat and then stir in the onion, cook it for 5 minutes with the heat up high to brown it at the edges, then remove it to a plate. Now, still on a high heat, brown the steak and kidney moving it around the pan till it's also browned nicely. Then return the onion to the casserole, sprinkle in the herbs and flour, and stir to allow the flour to soak up the juices.

Next gradually add the water (with the mushroom ketchup and Worcestershire sauce), stirring all the time, and finally add the mushrooms and a good seasoning of salt and pepper. Now turn the heat down to its lowest setting and simmer (covered) very gently for 1–1¼ hours or until the meat is tender.

When it is cooked, divide the mixture in half and spoon one half-quantity into a bowl, leave to get cold, then cover the bowl with clingfilm and place in the fridge until needed. Your other half-quantity is ready for one of the following recipes.

For the suet-crust topping:

1 oz shredded suet (25 g)

2 oz self-raising flour (50 g)

¼ teaspoon mixed herbs

water to mix

For this you'll need a 5 inch (13 cm) ramekin dish

Preheat the oven to gas mark 6, 400°F, 200°C. Then when your steak-and-kidney mixture is ready, make the pastry for the topping by simply stirring the suet and flour and herbs together in a bowl (no need to use your hands). Then add just enough cold water to bring it together to make a smooth pliable dough. Roll this into a ball then press it down on a working surface to make a flat disc-shape to fit the top of the ramekin (i.e. 5 inches, 13 cm, in diameter).

Now put your half-quantity of steak-and-kidney into the ramekin. Dampen the rim of the dish, then fit the disc of pastry on top, pressing it down well all round the edge to seal. Make a steam-hole, approximately the size of a 5p piece in the centre of the pastry, brush it all over with some milk, then bake on a high shelf in the oven for 25 minutes or until the pastry is golden and crusty.

Steak and kidney with puréed vegetable topping

This is part two, if you like, of the Mixed Double recipe on page 90. You use the reserved half of the steak-and-kidney mixture and top it with a layer of creamed vegetables before finishing off under the grill.

½ **quantity of the steak and kidney mixture** (*page 90*)
4 oz swede, after peeling (110 g)
4 oz potato, after peeling (110 g)
½ oz butter (10 g)
salt and freshly milled black pepper

You'll also need a 5 inch, 13 cm (diameter) ramekin dish

First of all cut the peeled vegetables into fairly large chunks, then place them in a saucepan with a little salt and just enough water to cover them. Cook them with the lid on for 7–8 minutes or until they are tender, then drain them in a colander. Now melt the butter in the saucepan the vegetables were cooked in, then return the drained swede and potato to the pan with a seasoning of salt and pepper. Then mash them until completely smooth.

While the vegetables are cooking, transfer the reserved steak-and-kidney mixture to another pan, and reheat very gently. Meanwhile preheat the grill and, when the mashed vegetables and the steak-and-kidney are ready, spoon the meat into the ramekin dish then spread the vegetables on top, levelling off with a fork by drawing it across the surface both ways. Place the dish under the grill just long enough for the topping to be tinged with flecks of brown.

Braised steak au poivre

This is an adaptation of the famous French classic, but more economical because it's made with braising steak. It does take longer to cook but it will simmer happily unattended, and there's very little work involved. The flavour is superb!

6–7 oz braising steak (175–200 g), in one or two pieces
1 small onion, chopped small
¾ teaspoon whole black peppercorns (or if you like it hotter, use 1 teaspoon)
1 dessertspoon oil
1 heaped teaspoon flour
1 small clove of garlic, crushed
4 fl oz red wine or dry cider (110 ml)
1 dessertspoon cream
salt

For this you need a small flameproof casserole with a well fitting lid so that the meat can cook on top of the stove. If you haven't got this, a small frying-pan with any lid that fits comfortably over the meat will do instead.

First heat the oil in the casserole and fry the onion in it for 5 minutes. While that's happening prepare the meat: crush the peppercorns with a pestle and mortar (or with the back of a tablespoon on a flat surface) – they need to be coarsely crushed. Next mix the crushed peppercorns with the flour on a flat plate and spread the mixture out evenly. Press the meat on to the mixture to get the underside well coated, then turn it over and do the same with the other side, pressing and patting the flour and pepper firmly into the meat.

Now remove the onion to a small plate, turn the heat right up and when it's really hot quickly brown the meat on both sides, scraping any flour-and-pepper from the plate into the casserole as well. Then turn the heat down, return the onion together with the garlic and some salt, pour in the wine, then put the lid on and let it simmer – as gently as possible – for 1¼ to 1½ hours, depending on the thickness of the steak. When it's ready, remove the lid, turn the heat right up and let the sauce bubble and reduce to a more syrupy consistency (about 1–2 minutes). Then stir in the cream till it's thoroughly blended – and that's it. Lovely with creamy mashed potatoes.

Beef curry cooked in yoghurt

A meat curry for one? Well, why not? By the time it's cooked your kitchen will have a marvellous spicy aroma, you'll be ravenous – and you'll really appreciate it.

8 oz chuck steak (225 g), cut into cubes
1 dessertspoon oil
1 small onion, chopped
¼ teaspoon cumin seeds
¼ teaspoon coriander seeds
1 cardamom pod
1 clove of garlic, crushed
½ teaspoon chopped fresh root ginger
1 teaspoon turmeric
½ teaspoon crushed dried chilli or chilli powder
3 tablespoons natural yoghurt
2½ fl oz water (60 ml)
½ oz grated creamed coconut (10 g)
salt

First heat the oil up in a small casserole, then add the onion and cook over a medium heat to soften for 5 minutes. Next turn the heat up high, add the cubes of meat and brown them on all sides, stirring them round the casserole.

Now crush the cumin and coriander seeds with the cardamom pod, using a pestle and mortar (or else a bowl and the end of a rolling-pin), and add them to the meat. Then stir in the garlic, ginger, turmeric and chilli, and cook for a minute or so before adding the yoghurt and water. Season with a little salt, then give everything a good stir to get it properly blended.

Put a lid on the casserole, then with the heat at the lowest possible simmer cook the curry for 1½ hours, giving it a stir from time to time to make sure it isn't sticking. When the time's up, stir in the creamed coconut, put the lid back on and cook (still very gently) for another 10–15 minutes. Test the meat with a skewer to make sure it is tender and taste to check the seasoning. Then serve with rice and mango chutney.

Oriental lamb

This has a very mild spicy flavour, and you can make it either with three lamb cutlets, two loin chops, or one decent-sized chump chop, depending on your preference and your appetite.

lamb chops (as above)
olive oil
½ teaspoon mixed spice
½ teaspoon curry powder
1 rounded tablespoon sultanas
½ teacup long-grain rice
1 small onion, chopped small
1 small clove of garlic, crushed
½ teaspoon turmeric
1 bayleaf
1 clove
1 small piece of cinnamon, approx 1 inch, 2·5 cm
1 teacup hot water
1 small banana
salt and freshly milled black pepper

Start off by mixing 1 tablespoon of olive oil with the mixed spice and curry powder in a cup, then spread this mixture on both sides of the chop(s) and leave in a cool spot for a while for the meat to absorb the flavours.

Next pour some boiling water over the sultanas and leave them, too, to stand for a while and plump up a bit.

Now for the rice. Heat one dessertspoon of oil in a small saucepan, then soften the onion and garlic in it for a couple of minutes before stirring in the rice and turmeric. Add the bayleaf, clove and cinnamon stick together with a seasoning of salt. Add the water, then put a lid on and simmer for 15 minutes or until all the liquid has been absorbed and the grains are tender.

Meanwhile smear a little oil in a thick-based frying-pan and fry the chop(s) for about 5 minutes on each side, depending on the thickness. Towards the end of the cooking, peel the banana, cut it into rounds and add them to the pan to fry a little on both sides. Now drain the sultanas, add these to the cooked rice and fork them into it (you can discard the clove and cinnamon). Serve the chops and fried banana on the bed of rice and serve with mango chutney.

Baked lamb with potato, garlic and rosemary

This recipe enables you to cook the meat and the potato together at the same time. I like to use an oval heatproof gratin dish for it – but a very small roasting tin would do as well.

2 loin lamb chops, trimmed
1 medium potato weighing approx 6 oz (175 g)
1 level teaspoon fresh rosemary
1 small clove of garlic
1 dessertspoon oil
1 small onion, chopped
2 ripe red tomatoes, peeled and chopped, or 2 level tablespoons tinned chopped Italian tomatoes
salt and freshly milled black pepper

Preheat the oven to gas mark 5, 375°F, 190°C
For this you need a 9 inch (23 cm) flameproof gratin dish

First of all peel the potato and cut it into small (½ inch, 5 mm) cubes, then put the cubes in a clean tea-cloth and dry them as thoroughly as possible. The rosemary should be crushed or bruised with a pestle and mortar, then finely chopped.

Next peel the garlic and cut a few slivers off; then, using a sharp knife, make a few little pockets in the chops and insert a sliver of garlic into each one (the rest of the garlic should be chopped small). Now place the gratin dish on a high heat and heat the oil in it. As soon as it's hot add the cubes of potato, the onion and the chopped garlic and toss them around in the hot oil.

Then make two spaces amongst the potato etc, and sit the chops in them. Sprinkle half the rosemary over the chops and the rest over the potatoes. Season everything with salt and pepper, then transfer the gratin dish to the high shelf in the oven to bake (uncovered) for about 25 minutes.

After that remove the dish, spoon the chopped tomatoes into the potatoes, and return to the oven for a further 5 minutes. Then serve the chops with the potato mixture spooned over them.

Right: Braised steak au poivre, page 93; Pork chop with apples and cider, page 112.

Piquant liver with sherry sauce

I used to make this with paper-thin slices of lambs liver, but it's so hard to get it cut thinly nowadays that I've switched to making it with chunks of liver cut into thin strips. This is lovely with creamed potatoes and fried cabbage.

6 oz lambs liver (175 g)
1 smallish onion, cut into rings
¾ teaspoon whole black peppercorns
½ rounded teaspoon flour
½ rounded teaspoon mustard powder
½ oz butter (10 g)
1 teaspoon oil
3 fl oz dry sherry or you could use wine or cider (75 ml)
½ teaspoon Worcestershire sauce
1 dessertspoon lemon juice
cayenne pepper
salt

First crush the peppercorns, either with a pestle and mortar or using the back of a tablespoon on a flat surface. You want them coarsely crushed – not as fine as through a peppermill. Then mix them in a small bowl with the flour and mustard powder.

Now heat the butter and oil in a 7 inch (18 cm) frying-pan and when it's hot fry the onion rings for about 10 minutes to get nicely browned round the edges. Then transfer the onion rings to a warmed serving dish and keep them warm.

Next quickly fry the liver pieces – when the blood begins to run, flip them over quickly to brown on the other side. It's most important not to overcook them: they should still be slightly pink inside. Then transfer the liver to join the onions and keep them warm.

Now stir the pepper, flour and mustard mixture into the juices left in the pan (if they seem to be lacking, add a knob of butter first). Stir to soak up all the juices, then gradually stir in the sherry followed by the Worcestershire sauce and lemon juice. If the sauce seems too thick, thin it with a drop of water (vegetable-cooking water would be good). Season with salt and a good pinch of cayenne, then pour over the liver and onion and serve straightaway.

Left: Chinese stir-fried chicken with broccoli and mushrooms, page 110; Chicken tikka kebab, page 108.

Lamb chops baked with aubergines

This one has a decidedly Greek flavour with its hint of cinnamon and oregano. Since both meat and vegetables are cooked together, it's an easy dish to prepare – but it's also rich, so needs only plain boiled potatoes or pilaff rice to go with it.

2 loin lamb chops, trimmed of most of their fat
1 smallish aubergine weighing approx 7 oz (200 g)
1 tablespoon olive oil
1 smallish onion, roughly chopped
1 clove of garlic, crushed
½ teaspoon oregano
a pinch of powdered cinnamon, ⅛ teaspoon
2 ripe tomatoes, peeled and chopped, or 2 heaped dessertspoons of chopped tinned Italian tomatoes
1 teaspoon chopped parsley
salt and freshly milled black pepper

Preheat the oven to gas mark 5, 375°F, 190°C

First prepare the aubergine. You need to get rid of some of its excess juice, so slice it in quarters lengthways then slice each quarter in two lengthways and finally cut these across into ½ inch (1 cm) pieces. Now spread them out on a plate, sprinkle them with about a teaspoon of salt, and then toss them around in the salt. Place them in a colander, press them down with a small plate and weight this down with a heavy scale-weight or something similar. Leave for 20 minutes, then transfer the aubergine pieces to a clean tea-cloth, squeezing each handful to extract as much of the juice as possible – then dry them in the cloth.

Now heat the oil in a small flameproof casserole and fry the onion in it for 5 minutes, then add the aubergine pieces and fry these, stirring them around in the oil until they begin to colour. Next add the garlic, oregano and cinnamon. Stir and cook for a few more seconds before adding the tomatoes. Mix everything together and season well with salt and pepper.

Next, sit the lamb chops on top of the vegetables, season and brush them with a little oil from the vegetables, then place the casserole (without a lid) in the oven for about 30 minutes – or until the lamb is cooked to your liking. Then serve the chops with the aubergines spooned over and a sprinkling of fresh chopped parsley.

Kofta kebab

These are little sausage-shaped kebabs of spiced minced lamb. For this you need to get a lamb steak.

8 oz lamb (225 g)
⅓ teaspoon cumin seeds
⅓ teaspoon coriander seeds
1 heaped dessertspoon freshly chopped mint
a little oil
salt and freshly milled black pepper

For the garnish: thin slivers of onion
lemon quarter

First prepare the meat by mincing it finely, incorporating all the fat as well as the lean as this helps to keep the kebabs moist while they're cooking. You can either mince the lamb through the fine blade of a mincer or else chop it finely in a food processor.

Place the minced meat in a bowl and season with salt and pepper. Now crush the cumin and coriander seeds as finely as possible with a pestle and mortar (or use the end of a rolling-pin and a basin) then add them to the meat together with the chopped mint. Mix everything together thoroughly, then cover the bowl with clingfilm and leave in a cool place for a while for the flavours to develop.

When you're ready to cook, preheat the grill. Take pieces of the meat mixture – approximately the size of a small egg – and roll them into rounds with the palms of your hands, then shape them into roughly sausage shapes. Thread them onto a flat skewer but don't pack them too closely, then brush each with a little oil. Place the kebab under the grill quite close to the heat and cook for 15–20 minutes, turning the skewer from time to time, until the meat is cooked and the outside nicely browned. Serve with pilaff rice (*page 135*).

Cider-braised pork with cream and mushrooms

This works very well on top of the stove in a small flame-proof casserole – or you could use a heavy-based frying-pan as long as you have some sort of close-fitting lid to place on top of it.

1 loin pork chop weighing 6–8 oz (175–225 g)
½ oz butter (10 g)
1 teaspoon oil
1 onion, chopped small
1 small clove of garlic, crushed
2 oz mushrooms (50 g), sliced
⅛ teaspoon crushed, chopped rosemary leaves
⅛ teaspoon chopped thyme, fresh or dried
3 fl oz dry cider (75 ml)
1 dessertspoon cream
salt and freshly milled black pepper

Begin by seasoning the pork chop with salt and pepper, then heat the butter and oil in your casserole till foaming and sizzling, and brown the chop to a nice golden colour on both sides. Then, using a draining spoon, remove it to a plate and keep on one side.

Now add the onion, garlic and mushrooms to the juices left in the pan and cook these together for about 5 minutes, then move them over to one side of the pan and return the chop. Sprinkle it with the herbs then spoon the mushroom and onion mixture over the top.

Pour in the cider, then turn the heat down to the lowest possible simmer. Cover and simmer gently for 30 minutes. After that turn the heat up and add the cream. Let it bubble and reduce very slightly (with the lid off), then serve the chop with the sauce poured over. This is excellent with quick stir-fried red cabbage (*see page 177*).

Porc au poivre

For this recipe the longer the pork chop can be marinated in garlic, oil and crushed pepper the better. So ideally you could prepare this the night before you need it. Otherwise the minimum marinating time is about 45 minutes (turning it over once during that time).

1 thick pork chop weighing 6–8 oz (175–225 g)
1 level teaspoon black peppercorns (or less if you don't like it too hot)
1 tablespoon olive oil
1 small clove of garlic, crushed
salt

For the sauce:

2 tablespoons red wine or white wine or even cider
1 tablespoon cream

First wipe the chop with kitchen paper to dry the surface. Now, using the pestle and mortar, crush the peppercorns – not too finely, they need to be fairly coarse. (If you don't have a pestle and mortar, you can achieve the same result by pressing the peppercorns hard under a tablespoon – provided you're prepared to crawl on all fours to collect the escapees!)

Next press half the crushed peppercorns as evenly as possible over one side of the chop, then turn it over and give the other side the same treatment. Now spoon the olive oil and crushed garlic into a shallow dish, then press the coated chop into the oil and turn it over so both sides get a coating of oil. Cover the dish loosely with foil then leave the chop to marinate, turning it over once during the time.

When you're ready to cook, scrape any oil from the dish into a 7 inch (18 cm) heavy-based frying-pan, and heat it to very hot. Season the chop with salt, then add the chop to the pan to brown quickly on both sides. After that turn the heat down to medium and let the chop cook for about 10 minutes on each side (depending on its thickness). As soon as it is done, pour in the wine and let it bubble and reduce for about 20 seconds before stirring the cream into the pan juices. Serve immediately with the sauce poured over.

Barbecued pork slices

Lean belly pork strips are much more economical than chops or fillet – so if you're not in a hurry or don't want to eat as soon as you get home, give this a try. It takes an hour, and you could pop a jacket potato in the oven to cook alongside it.

8 oz belly pork strips (225 g)
1 small onion, chopped finely
1 teaspoon oil
salt and freshly milled black pepper

For the marinade:

2 tablespoons dry cider or white wine
1 tablespoon soy sauce
1 level teaspoon mustard powder
½ level teaspoon powdered ginger
1 heaped teaspoon soft brown sugar

Preheat the oven to gas mark 6, 400°F, 200°C

First of all oil a heatproof shallow 7 inch (18 cm) gratin dish and lay the pork slices in it, brushing them with a little oil as well. Scatter the chopped onion over and in amongst the slices, add a little seasoning then bake in the oven for 20 minutes.

Next simply mix the marinade ingredients together in a small jug and, after the 20 minutes cooking is up, pour the sauce all over the pork slices. Return them to the oven and bake for a further 25–30 minutes, basting the meat with the sauce two or three times during that period. This is also good with onion rice (*see page 134*) and the quick stir-fried red cabbage (*see page 177*).

Stuffed pork chop with fennel

This particular stuffing gives the chop an unusual and distinctive flavour – decidedly a change from the traditional sage and onion.

1 thick pork chop weighing 7–8 oz (200–225 g)
½ oz butter (10 g)
1 small onion, chopped
½ or 1 small clove of garlic, crushed
1 dessertspoon of chopped celery
1 dessertspoon fresh chopped parsley
⅓ teaspoon fennel seeds, crushed with pestle and mortar
1 dessertspoon fresh brown breadcrumbs
1 dessertspoon oil
1 dessertspoon flour seasoned with salt and pepper
3 fl oz dry cider or dry white wine (75 ml)
1 tablespoon cream
salt and freshly milled black pepper

In a small, heavy-based casserole melt the butter and soften the onion and garlic in it for 5 minutes. Meanwhile place the celery, parsley, fennel seeds and breadcrumbs in a small bowl, then tip in the onion and garlic and all the buttery juices to join them in the bowl, season with salt and pepper, then mix thoroughly.

Now, using a sharp knife, cut a sort of pocket in the chop horizontally, then pack as much stuffing as you can into it (the rest can go on top later). In the same casserole heat the oil, then dust the chop on both sides with seasoned flour to brown it quickly on both sides to a crusty golden-brown.

Next spoon off the excess oil from the casserole and spread the rest of the stuffing on top of the pork chop. Pour in the cider or wine, turn the heat down to the gentlest possible simmer, put a lid on and let it simmer for 30 minutes. Towards the end of the cooking time, preheat the grill, then remove the lid from the casserole, spoon the cream over the chop and pop it under the grill for a minute or two to brown a little. Serve with all the casserole juices spooned over.

Hung shao pork

The utter simplicity of this slow-cooked Chinese pork dish is as much a joy as its flavour. What gives it this is a spice called star anise, which looks like a star-shaped piece of cinnamon bark: if you have trouble locating it, you can buy it by post (see page 214).

½ lb lean pork belly strips, including the skin (225 g)

2 tablespoons soy sauce

1 dessertspoon water

1 level teaspoon finely chopped fresh root ginger

½ piece star anise

1 inch whole cinnamon stick (2·5 cm)

½ teaspoon sugar

1½ tablespoons sherry

salt

For the garnish: 1 finely chopped spring onion

First cut the pork into 1 inch (2·5 cm) cubes, making sure each piece has some of the skin as this is very important for the flavour of the dish. Next arrange the pieces skin-side down in a small flameproof casserole, sprinkle with salt, then with the soy sauce and the water. Now add the chopped ginger to the pork and pop the star anise and cinnamon in, too.

Cover the casserole and let the pork cook over the lowest possible heat on top of the stove for 45 minutes. After that turn the pieces of pork over, sprinkle in the sugar, and add the sherry. Cover again and cook for a further 45 minutes, turning the meat over once or twice more during that time. Serve the pork with the juices poured over.

Baked Hungarian pork chop

If you're not in too much of a hurry this is a little gem for a cold winter's night. The preparation time is minimal, but it does take forty-five minutes to cook in the oven.

1 thick pork chop weighing 6–8 oz (175–225 g)
1 teaspoon groundnut oil
1 potato (approx 7 oz, 200 g)
1 small onion, very thinly sliced
a pinch of cayenne
1 rounded teaspoon hot paprika
1 pinch of caraway seeds
a knob of butter
2½ fl oz soured cream (65 ml) or 2 tablespoons of single cream mixed with 1 tablespoon of yoghurt
salt and freshly milled black pepper

Preheat the oven to gas mark 5, 375°F, 190°C

This fits perfectly into a cast-iron enamelled gratin dish (9 inches maximum length × 5½ inches wide, 23 × 14 cm) but a small roasting tin would also do. While the oven is preheating, put the oil in the gratin dish and pop it into the oven to preheat as well.

Meanwhile peel and slice the potato and the onion as thinly as possible. Now, on a flat plate, combine the cayenne and paprika with some salt and pepper, then dry the chop thoroughly with some kitchen paper and coat it on each side with this mixture.

Remove the dish from the oven, and arrange first the sliced onion and then the sliced potato over the base, then place the pork chop on top. Sprinkle it with caraway seeds and place a knob of butter on top. Bake in the top of the oven for 30 minutes. After that pour the cream over and bake for a further 15 minutes. This is nice served with some quick stir-fried red cabbage (*see page 177*).

Chicken chasseur

This is chicken cooked in red wine with tomato, herbs and mushrooms. It has a strongly reduced sauce which gives it a very pronounced flavour. The other nice thing about it is that it can all be made on top of the stove.

1 chicken quarter, leg and thigh joint
1 teaspoon flour
1 tablespoon oil
1 small onion, roughly chopped
1 clove of garlic, finely chopped
½ teaspoon fresh chopped thyme or ¼ teaspoon dried thyme
½ teaspoon bruised, chopped rosemary or ¼ teaspoon dried rosemary
4 fl oz red wine (110 ml)
4 tomatoes, peeled and chopped, or 4 dessertspoons of tinned chopped Italian tomatoes
1 bayleaf
2 oz dark-gilled mushrooms (50 g), cut into ½ inch (1 cm) pieces
salt and freshly milled black pepper

If you buy the chicken quarter in one piece, then divide it in two: place it skin-side up, stretch the leg as far as you can, and cut through the natural line dividing the leg from the rest. Season with salt and pepper and dust each piece with flour, then in a small flameproof casserole (or thick-based saucepan) heat the oil.

When the oil is hot brown the chicken joints on all sides in it, then remove them to a plate. Next add the onion and garlic to the casserole, fry these for 5 minutes or until pale gold. Then stir in the herbs, followed by the wine and tomatoes. Bring it all up to simmering point, then return the chicken pieces and pop in the bayleaf.

Put a tight-fitting lid on, and simmer as gently as possible for 40 minutes. After that take off the lid and turn the chicken pieces over, and add the mushrooms (pushing them well down into the sauce). Carry on gently simmering (without a lid) for about 10 minutes. Then remove the chicken pieces to a serving dish to keep warm.

Turn the heat up and let the sauce bubble and reduce for about 3–4 minutes until it's thick and concentrated. Taste to check the seasoning. Simply pour the sauce over the chicken and serve with rice.

Poached breast of chicken with cream and mushrooms

In the summer half a teaspoon of fresh chopped tarragon leaves would be ideal for this, if you can get any. If not, half a teaspoon of dried tarragon will do.

1 chicken breast or other chicken joint
6 fl oz dry white wine or dry cider (175 ml)
1 oz mushrooms (25 g), sliced
a good pinch of dried tarragon (or fresh – see above)
1 egg yolk
1 tablespoon cream
salt and freshly milled black pepper

In a medium-sized saucepan bring the wine up to simmering point, then add the chicken breast together with some salt and freshly milled pepper. Bring back up to simmering point, put a lid on, and simmer gently for 15 minutes (or 30 minutes if not a breast). Then remove the chicken and keep it warm (if you've not got a warming section in your oven, you can keep it warm by placing it on a serving plate on top of a pan of barely simmering water).

Now add the mushrooms and tarragon to the cooking liquid and boil it quite fast (without a lid) until it has reduced in volume by about a half, and then remove it from the heat. Now in a small basin beat together the egg yolk and cream, and mix a couple of tablespoons of the hot cooking-liquid into the egg mixture, then pour the whole mixture back in to join the rest in the saucepan.

Return the pan to a low heat and, stirring all the time, reheat it until it thickens. Don't, whatever you do, let it come to the boil or it will separate! As soon as it's thickened, pour it over the chicken and serve.

Chicken tikka kebab

These are little chicken kebabs, marinated in a spicy yoghurt mixture for several hours – after which they almost melt in the mouth!

1 chicken breast weighing approx 6 oz (175 g)

For the marinade:

2 tablespoons natural yoghurt

¼ teaspoon cumin seeds

¼ teaspoon coriander seeds

1 cardamom pod

½ teaspoon turmeric

1 clove of garlic, crushed

½ teaspoon grated root ginger

¼ teaspoon chilli powder

¼ teaspoon salt

Begin by making up the marinade mixture. Measure the yoghurt into a bowl, then crush the cumin and coriander seeds together with the cardamom pod in a pestle and mortar (failing that, use the end of a rolling-pin and a basin) and add them to the yoghurt. After that add the rest of the marinade ingredients and stir well to get everything thoroughly combined.

Now cut the chicken breast into medium-sized chunks (you should get about six or seven) then add them to the marinade and stir again to get the chicken pieces properly coated. Cover the bowl with clingfilm and leave in the refrigerator for at least 3–4 hours to marinate. You could, if you wanted to, start this off the night before.

When you're ready to cook, preheat the grill to high. Then thread the pieces of chicken onto a skewer, if possible a flat one, which makes it so much easer to turn the kebabs. Don't pack them too tightly, give them room for the heat to get to them. If any of the chicken pieces are flat rather than chunky, fold them over before threading them.

Now set the skewer so that the ends rest on the side of a gratin dish (or similar shallow dish) to make sure any juice drips into the dish and not the grill. Now drizzle a little oil over the chicken pieces and place the dish under the grill so that the chicken is 1–2 inches (2·5–5 cm) from the heat. Grill for 10–15 minutes, turning the skewer a couple of times, or until the spicy crust has charred a bit all over and the chicken pieces are cooked through. Serve on a bed of rice (cooked perhaps with a little onion and pepper) and some mango chutney.

Chicken in paprika sauce

For one person this is good made with a leg and thigh portion cut into two small joints. I would recommend serving it with rice or buttered noodles to soak up the sauce.

1 chicken joint
1 dessertspoon olive oil
1 small onion, chopped
1 clove of garlic, crushed
1 heaped teaspoon paprika
a good pinch of cayenne
7 oz tin of Italian tomatoes or 7 oz, 200 g, red ripe tomatoes, skinned and chopped
½ green pepper, chopped
1 tablespoon natural yoghurt or cream
salt and freshly milled black pepper

In a small flameproof casserole heat the oil to very hot, then season the chicken portion(s) and brown them in the hot oil to a good golden colour. Then remove them to a plate.

Next add the onion and garlic to the casserole and brown these till softened and golden (about 5 minutes). Next stir the paprika and cayenne into the onion and return the chicken pieces, then pour in the tomatoes. Bring everything up to simmering point, cover and simmer very gently for 30 minutes.

After that remove the lid and add the chopped pepper, pushing it down into the sauce, then just carry on simmering (this time without a lid) until the pepper is softened and cooked and the sauce has reduced down to a good thick consistency (about 20–25 minutes). Before serving, taste to check the seasoning and stir the yoghurt or cream into the sauce to give it a lovely marbled effect.

Gammon steak with honey and mustard sauce

This is so quick and effort-less – and proves that simplic-ity is so often the best. Excellent served with the quick stir-fried cabbage (see page 177).

1 gammon steak weighing 6–8 oz (175–225 g)
1 tablespoon runny honey
2 teaspoons Dijon mustard
1 teaspoon English mustard
½ oz butter (10 g)
freshly milled black pepper

To prevent the gammon from curling up while it's cooking, just snip the fat at about 1 inch (2·5 cm) intervals all round. Then combine all the ingredients for the sauce – the honey, mustard and a few twists of pepper – in a bowl.

Now put a small roasting tin (or gratin dish) containing the butter under the grill and heat the butter until it starts to sizzle. Then remove the dish from the heat and pour in the honey-mustard mixture, stirring to combine it with the butter.

Next take the gammon slice and drag it through the mixture and lay it – sauced side up – in the tin or dish and grill about 6 inches (15 cm) from the heat for 5 minutes on each side.

Chinese stir-fried chicken with broccoli and mushrooms

Chinese-style recipes are often perfect for one, because many of them are made at top speed. The trouble is that westerners are often inclined to add a little extra cooking time, and the end-result can be just that little bit overdone. How-ever practice makes perfect and after you've made this a few times you'll soon learn to get just the right amount of bite and crispness.

1 small chicken breast weighing approx 6 oz (175 g)
1½ oz broccoli or calabrese florets (40 g)
3 oz mushrooms (75 g), cut in slices through the stalks
1 dessertspoon cornflour
1 dessertspoon soy sauce
1½ tablespoons oil
1 small onion, chopped small
1 clove of garlic, chopped
1 teaspoon grated fresh root ginger
½ teaspoon salt
2 tablespoons sherry mixed with 1 tablespoon water
2 spring onions, finely chopped

First of all remove the skin and any bone from the chicken breast, and cut it into small pieces (approx 1 × ½ inch, 2·5 × 1 cm). Then place the pieces in a small bowl, sprinkle them with the cornflour and mix well, using your hands, until all the pieces are well coated. Next sprinkle in the soy sauce and mix again until they've all been coated with that too. Cover the bowl and leave it in a cool place for 30 minutes.

After that, heat 1 tablespoon of oil in a 7 inch (18 cm) frying-pan and when it's very hot stir-fry the chicken pieces for about two minutes, keeping them on the move and tossing them about all the time so that all sides get into contact with the heat. Then remove them to a plate and keep warm.

Next add ½ tablespoon of oil to the pan and add the chopped onion, garlic and ginger. Let that cook for about 2 minutes, then add the broccoli, mushrooms and salt – and stir-fry these, again tossing them all around over a high heat for about one minute.

Now return the chicken to the pan, turn the heat down to medium, pour in the sherry and water and sprinkle half the spring onion in. Put a lid on the pan and cook for a further minute. Serve straightaway then, with the rest of the spring onion sprinkled over.

Pork chop with apples and cider

I actually prefer dry cider to dry white wine for this particular recipe, as it enhances the apple flavour. I make this a sure candidate for my personal top-ten recipes for one.

1 nice thick pork chop weighing approx 7–8 oz (200–225 g)
1 small Cox's apple or very small Bramley (chopped small but with the skin left on)
1 small onion, chopped small
½ oz butter (10 g)
a little oil
4 fl oz dry cider (110 ml)
1 tablespoon single or double cream
salt and freshly milled black pepper

In a solid-based 7 inch (18 cm) frying-pan melt the butter together with a little oil added to prevent it browning too much. When it begins to foam, add the apple and onion, turn the heat to medium and cook these for about 5 minutes – they need to become a nice toasted golden colour round the edges.

Now, using a draining spoon, transfer the cooked apple and onion to a plate and keep on one side. Next season the pork chop with salt and pepper on both sides, turn the heat up under the frying-pan and cook the chop for about 10 minutes on each side (depending on the thickness), turning the heat down halfway through.

As soon as it is cooked, return the apple and onion to the pan, then pour in the cider and let it bubble and reduce to about half its original volume. Then stir in the cream. Serve the chop with the apple and onion piled on top and the sauce poured over.

Gammon steak with gherkin sauce

This is best made with the small sharply flavoured gherkins, and not the large fat dill cucumbers. This goes particularly well with the potatoes Niçoise (see page 180).

1 gammon steak weighing 6–8 oz (175–225 g)
1 small onion, finely chopped
½ oz butter (10 g)
1 rounded teaspoon flour
4 fl oz dry white wine or dry cider (110 ml)
2 or 3 gherkins, finely chopped – one dessertspoonful altogether
1 dessertspoon fresh chopped parsley
1 squeeze of lemon juice
salt and freshly milled black pepper

Preheat the grill, and while it's warming up make the sauce. In a small saucepan melt the butter and soften the onion in it for 5 minutes, then stir in the flour and gradually add the wine or cider, a little at a time, stirring after each addition until you have a smooth sauce. Turn the heat down to the lowest possible and let the sauce simmer for 10 minutes while you're cooking the gammon.

Remove the rind (the birds will love it chopped!) then snip the fat with kitchen scissors at 1 inch (2·5 cm) intervals all round – this helps to keep it flat while it's cooking. Grill the gammon for 2–3 minutes on each side depending on the thickness of the steak.

Towards the end of the cooking time stir the chopped gherkin, parsley and lemon juice into the sauce, then taste and season with pepper (but watch the salt because the gammon may be salty). Serve the gammon with the sauce poured over – and some nice sharp mustard would go well with it.

Fried chicken breast with cheese

The cheese you use for this can vary: a mild crumbly Wensleydale would be good or, if you prefer a highly flavoured cheese, try a Cheddar with Chives and Onion in it. It is good served with a green salad with lots of watercress in it.

1 chicken breast
1 oz grated cheese (25 g)
1 tablespoon flour seasoned with salt and pepper
1 small egg, beaten
1 heaped tablespoon fresh breadcrumbs
groundnut oil for deep-frying
salt and freshly milled black pepper

First of all pour enough oil into a medium saucepan to come halfway up, and start to heat it. Meanwhile, using a very sharp knife, cut a pocket on the inside of the chicken breast and fill the pocket with the grated cheese.

Now dust the chicken with seasoned flour, then coat it first in beaten egg and then roll the chicken in breadcrumbs, pressing them in firmly all round to get an even coating.

Test the oil – it will be hot enough when a small cube of bread sizzles and turns golden-brown in 1 minute. Now lower the chicken into the oil and, keeping the heat at medium, cook it for about 10 minutes. Then remove it with a draining spoon onto crumpled greaseproof paper to drain well. Before serving, sprinkle with salt and freshly milled black pepper.

Chicken breast with preserved ginger sauce

Preserved ginger is a wonderful storecupboard standby, because it keeps indefinitely and there's never any waste. This is good served with brown rice cooked with onion, and a crisp salad.

1 chicken breast
1 dessertspoon preserved ginger syrup
½ teaspoon freshly grated root ginger
1 piece of preserved ginger, chopped
1 tablespoon oil
1 small onion, chopped small
1 small clove of garlic, crushed
a knob of butter
2 tablespoons dry white wine or dry cider
1 dessertspoon natural yoghurt
1 spring onion, finely chopped
salt and freshly milled black pepper

Preheat the oven to gas mark 5, 375°F, 190°C

Start off by heating the oil in a medium-sized saucepan and soften the onion and garlic in it for about 5 minutes. Meanwhile place the chicken joint in a flameproof gratin dish or small roasting tin, then pierce it with a skewer or small sharp knife in several places (this is to allow the ginger to seep down inside).

Now spoon the ginger syrup over the joint, rubbing it in with your hands. Next sprinkle the freshly grated root ginger over and rub that in as well. Season the chicken with salt and pepper, then pour the onion (and oil) from the saucepan over, and place a knob of butter on top.

Bake the chicken in the oven for about 40 minutes, basting it with the juices about halfway through. When it's cooked, remove the chicken to a warmed serving plate, then place the cooking dish (or tin) over direct heat on top of the stove. Add the wine and chopped ginger, and let it bubble down to a syrupy sauce. Then, off the heat, stir in the yoghurt. Pour the sauce over the chicken and sprinkle with chopped spring onion.

Chicken Véronique

Another little treasure, this one, which I think goes particularly well with plain buttered noodles.

1 quarter chicken joint (leg and thigh) weighing approx 6 oz (175 g)
½ oz butter (10 g)
1 small onion, chopped
½ teaspoon tarragon, fresh or dried
4 fl oz dry white wine (110 ml)
2 oz white grapes (50 g), halved and depipped
1 tablespoon cream
salt and freshly milled black pepper

For the thickening:

½ teaspoon butter and ½ teaspoon flour worked together to a paste

In a small saucepan melt the butter, season the chicken joint with salt and pepper and cook it in the hot butter till golden on both sides (approximately 5 minutes), then remove it to a plate.

Now add the onion to the pan and cook that for about 5 minutes also, or until softened, then return the chicken joint and sprinkle the tarragon over. Pour in the wine, cover the pan with a tight lid, and simmer very gently for 30 minutes or until the chicken is tender – the length of the cooking time will depend on its size.

After that remove the lid and turn the heat up. Let the sauce bubble and reduce slightly for about a minute, then whisk in the butter and flour paste till the sauce has thickened a bit and then turn the heat down and add the halved grapes and stir in the cream. Allow them to heat through, then taste and check the seasoning, and serve the chicken with the sauce poured over.

Poulet Basque

offered this recipe and added 'every meal should be a festival, so why should I make myself the exception?'

1 breast of chicken weighing approx 8 oz (225 g)
brown rice measured to the 3 fl oz level in a glass measuring jug (75 ml)
1 medium onion, finely chopped
½ green or red pepper, finely chopped
3 ripe tomatoes, skinned and chopped, or 3 tablespoons of Italian chopped tomatoes
½ oz butter (10 g)
2 dessertspoons olive oil
seasoned flour
1 clove of garlic, crushed
½ teaspoon dried basil
4 black olives, stoned and chopped
1 slice of orange, approx ¾ oz (20 g)
salt and freshly milled black pepper

This recipe comes from my friend, Ken Toye, in whose restaurant I started my cooking career many years ago. It was called The Singing Chef and in those days it was in London. Now, to my great delight, he has opened up near us in Ipswich. When I asked him what he cooked for himself when he was on his own, he

Start off by heating the butter and 1 dessertspoon of oil in a frying-pan. Then coat the chicken breast in the seasoned flour, and add it to the pan to brown nicely on all sides. Use a draining spoon to transfer the chicken breast to a small saucepan and pour in just enough water to cover. Season with salt and simmer gently (covered) for 20 minutes.

While that's happening, add another dessertspoon of oil to the frying-pan, then add the chopped onion and pepper and cook to soften for 5 minutes or so. Next add the rice and stir well; add the garlic and a good seasoning of salt and pepper, then pour in ½ pint (275 ml) of boiling water. Cover the pan (with a lid or a suitably sized plate) and simmer gently for 20 minutes.

After 20 minutes, add the basil, the chopped olives, the slice of orange (cut in half) and the chopped tomatoes. Stir to incorporate these into the rice, then place the cooked chicken in the rice. If at this stage the rice is dry, add a couple of tablespoons of hot water, next cover the pan again and cook for a further 20 minutes (gently). Then serve straightaway.

Prime Pasta and Rice

For people in other parts of the world pasta and rice dishes have for centuries provided the means by which meat or fish can be supplemented and stretched. And the result has been some marvellously inventive dishes. For a long time in Britain we either simply put them into milk puddings, or else we confined rice to kedgeree or as an accompaniment to curry, while macaroni cheese was our only real claim to pasta.

The fact that pasta and rice dishes are now an integral part of our eating pattern is largely due to the postwar revolution in holiday travel. Ethnic restaurants in almost every town in the country have also played an important part in making us aware of the rich and wonderful range of recipes that can be made with pasta and rice. Pasta is now available in every shape and size, plain and wholewheat, even (I'm delighted to see) fresh in some supermarkets. My most recent revelation has been made researching in Chinese supermarkets – the whole range of noodles that can now be bought, including those delightfully light, transparent, rice noodles which need no cooking but just a few minutes soaking (*see page 21*).

Rice (which is also the subect of this chapter) is now available in all its varieties, too. Because I do think it's important to choose the right kind of rice for the right dish, I offer these few notes as a guideline:

For Indian dishes and curries generally *Basmati rice* with its long thin pointed grains is the best for both quality and flavour. I also choose this for serving with Chinese recipes and for making fried rice.

Easy-cook Italian rice is a good all-purpose rice: although this has been treated to remove some of the outer surface the grains, when cooked, are firm, slightly rounded and provide plenty of bite. This would be my choice for making paella (*see page 132*) if you can't track down the authentic Valencia rice.

For real risotto Italian *arborio rice* is the very best. Being untreated and more starchy, it produces the characteristic creaminess of the genuine risotto (*see page 129*).

Brown or wholegrain rice, having the bran and germ layers of the grain intact, is chewier and nuttier than white rice (and has more flavour). The best quality to buy is long-grain and the best variety I have come across is that packaged by Harmony Foods – followed closely by Sainsbury's own brand.

Green tagliatelle with three cheeses

If by any chance you are near a delicatessen or an Italian food shop that sells Ricotta cheese – do buy some because, with the Gorgonzola, it makes the perfect combination for this dish. Otherwise cottage cheese will make an excellent alternative. This is quick, simple and delicious.

4 oz green tagliatelle (110 g) (or 1 ounce more or less, according to appetite)
1½ oz Gorgonzola cheese (40 g)
2 oz cottage cheese or Ricotta (50 g)
1 small clove of garlic
3 tablespoons single cream
1 tablespoon olive oil
¼ red or green pepper, very finely chopped
2 spring onions, including the green parts, finely chopped
salt and freshly milled black pepper

Serve with: 1 dessertspoon freshly grated Parmesan

Place the pasta in a pan with plenty of boiling salted water (with a few drops of oil added to prevent it sticking), and when the water has returned to the boil cook for exactly 8 minutes.

Meanwhile you can be preparing the sauce: all you do is place the Gorgonzola cheese and cottage cheese (or Ricotta) in the goblet of a liquidiser together with the garlic, cream and half a tablespoon of hot water. Season with salt and pepper then blend until completely smooth.

When the tagliatelle is ready, drain it thoroughly in a colander, then return it immediately to the hot pan. Add the olive oil, chopped pepper and spring onions plus a seasoning of salt and pepper, then toss well. Now spoon the cheese mixture into the pasta, toss again thoroughly then serve straight onto a hot plate, and sprinkle with the Parmesan.

Pasta with creamed mushrooms and nutmeg

I'm giving this five stars for simplicity and flavour, and it's certainly one of those recipes that proves you don't always have to spend a lot of time and trouble if you want to avoid eating meat.

4–5 oz pasta (110–150 g) – I like to use half wholewheat spaghetti and half white spaghetti
4 oz dark open mushrooms (110 g), sliced
½ oz butter (10 g)
1 egg yolk
3 tablespoons double cream
2 rounded tablespoons freshly grated Parmesan cheese
⅛ whole nutmeg, grated
salt and freshly milled black pepper

In a medium-sized saucepan melt the butter, then stir in the mushrooms – it will look as if you've got far too many mushrooms for that amount of butter, but they'll soon collapse down. Stir them around quite a bit, then season with salt and pepper. Put a lid on the pan and, keeping the heat low, let the mushrooms sweat and release their juice for 5 minutes.

After that take the lid off and let them continue simmering gently so that the mushroom juices will reduce and their flavour will become more concentrated. This will take about 15 minutes – and your kitchen will be permeated with a very appetising mushroom aroma.

Meanwhile beat the egg yolk and cream together thoroughly, adding a tablespoon of Parmesan and ⅛ of a whole nutmeg grated. Cook the pasta in plenty of boiling salted water (with a drop or two of oil added to prevent it sticking together) for just 8 minutes, no longer. Drain in a colander, then return the pasta to the hot saucepan. Pour in the cream mixture immediately, followed by the mushrooms, stirring and lifting the pasta up with a spoon to distribute the mushrooms and sauce evenly. Serve on a hot plate with the rest of the Parmesan sprinkled over.

Note: a couple of presoaked dried mushrooms along with the fresh mushrooms would add extra flavour to this (*see page 20*).

Spaghetti in the Mediterranean style

I use spaghetti with this sauce, but that's optional. Green or white tagliatelle would also go well.

3–4 oz spaghetti (75–110 g) – or even 5 oz, 150 g, it depends on your appetite
1 small green pepper
1 tablespoon oil
1 small onion, chopped
4 oz tomatoes, fresh or tinned Italian (110 g)
1 small clove of garlic, crushed
¼ teaspoon oregano
1 teaspoon tomato purée
3 anchovy fillets, drained and chopped
1 dessertspoon capers, chopped
2 or 3 black olives, stoned and halved
salt and freshly milled black pepper

Serve with: plenty of freshly grated Parmesan

For this, the pepper is cooked Mediterranean-fashion under the grill. To do this you cut it into quarters, remove the seeds and lay the quarters (skin-side up) on the grill rack and cook them until they are black and blistered. Rinse them under the running tap and peel off the charred skins, then dry and chop the flesh into quite small pieces.

Next heat the oil in a 7 inch (18 cm) frying-pan and fry the onion for 5 minutes before adding the pepper, tomatoes, garlic, oregano and tomato purée. Continue to cook the sauce over a medium heat for about 10 minutes.

Towards the end of the cooking time boil the pasta for 8 minutes. Meanwhile finish off the sauce by adding the anchovies, capers and olives, then keep the heat low until the pasta is ready. When it is cooked, drain it in a colander, then return it to the saucepan and pour in the sauce, with a good seasoning of salt and pepper, and toss it all together. Then serve on a hot soup plate sprinkled generously with Parmesan.

Spaghetti with cream, egg and bacon

This is certainly one of the quickest recipes in the book, twelve minutes from start to finish the last time I made it! I'm equally certain it doesn't taste like it.

3–4 oz spaghetti (75–110 g), depending on your appetite
½ oz butter (10 g)
1 teaspoon oil
½ small onion, chopped small
2 oz streaky bacon (50 g), chopped into strips
1 egg
1 dessertspoon cream
salt and freshly milled black pepper

Serve with: freshly grated Parmesan

First put the spaghetti on to cook in a large pan, and cover with plenty of boiling salted water (with a few drops of oil added to prevent it sticking). Then boil it for just 8 minutes.

Meanwhile heat the butter and oil together in a frying-pan, then add the chopped onion and bacon and cook over a medium heat to soften for 5–7 minutes. And while that's happening beat the egg together with the cream in a small basin.

When the spaghetti is cooked – it should still be *al dente* as the Italians say, that is it should still have a bit of bite to it – drain it in a colander then return it to the hot saucepan. Now stir in the onion and bacon (plus all the buttery juices), then pour in the egg-and-cream mixture. Season with salt and pepper, then toss everything around the pan so it gets amalgamated with the pasta (the heat left in the pan will be enough to cook the egg to a coating-sauce consistency). Serve the spaghetti on a warmed plate and sprinkle with plenty of Parmesan.

Wholewheat noodles with mushrooms and Boursin cheese

Actually it doesn't have to be Boursin cheese: there's also one called Tartare, another called Cantadou, yet another called Roulé. All are cream cheeses with garlic and herbs – and that's what's needed.

3–4 oz wholewheat ribbon noodles (75–110 g) – or if you're very hungry, 5 oz (150 g)
1½ tablespoons olive oil
1 small onion, chopped
1 oz rasher of bacon (25 g), chopped
3 oz mushrooms (75 g), sliced
1 clove of garlic, crushed
1 rounded tablespoon fresh chopped parsley
2½ oz cream cheese with garlic and herbs (60 g)
1 tablespoon dry white breadcrumbs
1 tablespoon freshly grated Parmesan cheese
½ oz butter (10 g)
salt and freshly milled black pepper

First of all cook the noodles in plenty of boiling, salted water (with a few drops of oil added to prevent them sticking together) for 8 minutes – or if they happen to be fresh noodles 3–4 minutes will be enough. Meanwhile preheat the grill. Heat the oil in another pan and fry the onion and bacon in it for 5 minutes, then stir in the mushrooms and garlic and continue to cook over a fairly high heat for 3–4 minutes. Then turn the heat off under the pan, sprinkle in the parsley and season with salt and pepper.

Now quickly drain the noodles and transfer them to the pan containing the onion and mushrooms. Next add in the cream cheese, put the lid on and leave for a few minutes for the cheese to melt, then mix the contents of the pan.

Taste to check the seasoning, then transfer the noodles to a lightly buttered baking-dish. Mix the breadcrumbs and grated Parmesan together and sprinkle this over the top and dot the surface with flecks of butter. Brown under the grill for about 5 minutes, then serve immediately.

Note: a vegetarian could omit the bacon in this – it works perfectly well without it.

Spaghetti with Mexican sauce

To make this sauce you need the other half of the Mixed Double recipe on page 88, which will provide you with just the right quantity of cooked minced beef.

4–5 oz spaghetti (110–150 g), depending on your appetite
1 quantity of cooked minced beef
1 dessertspoon oil
1 small green pepper, finely chopped
1 large clove of garlic, crushed
1 heaped tablespoon tomato purée
2 tablespoons red wine or dry cider
¼ teaspoon crushed dried chilli or chilli powder
1 dessertspoon fresh chopped parsley
salt and plenty of grated Parmesan to sprinkle over

In a small saucepan heat the oil, then cook the chopped pepper in it for about 10 minutes to start softening. After that add the garlic, cook that for about a minute, then stir in the beef mixture along with the tomato purée, red wine, chilli powder and parsley. Stir everything well, then bring it up to simmering point and simmer for 10 minutes.

Meanwhile cook the spaghetti in plenty of boiling salted water (with a few drops of oil added to prevent it sticking) for 8 minutes. Then drain in a colander and serve straightaway on a warmed plate, with the sauce poured over, and freshly grated Parmesan sprinkled on top.

Tagliatelle Toscana

In this recipe the pasta along with the other ingredients – aubergines, tomatoes, Mozzarella amongst other things – are finished off for a few minutes in the oven. You could, however, use the grill instead if you keep an eye on it (see below).

1 medium-sized aubergine weighing 5–6 oz (150–175 g)
1 tablespoon olive oil
2 oz chopped onion (50 g)
6 oz ripe tomatoes (175 g), skinned and chopped, or else use tinned chopped Italian tomatoes
1 clove of garlic, crushed
½ level teaspoon dried basil
1 rounded dessertspoon tomato purée
2–3 black olives, stoned and chopped
2–3 oz tagliatelle (50–75 g), depending on your appetite
½ oz butter (10 g)
2 tablespoons grated Parmesan
2 oz Mozzarella cheese (40 g), diced
salt and freshly milled black pepper

Preheat the oven to gas mark 4, 350°F, 180°C

Note: You could also finish this off by placing the baking-dish for 10 minutes under a preheated grill 3–4 inches (7·5–10 cm) away from the heat. But you will have to keep an eye on it and if it browns too quickly, place a piece of foil loosely over the top and increase the time to 15 minutes.

Begin by dicing – but not peeling – the aubergine into approximately 1 inch (2·5 cm) dice, place these in a colander, sprinkle with salt, then cover them with a plate weighted down with scale-weights or similar. Leave them for 20 minutes then squeeze them dry in a clean tea-cloth (this is to get rid of their excess moisture).

Now heat the oil in a heavy-based pan and fry the onion gently in it to soften for 5 minutes before adding the drained aubergine. Carry on cooking for another 5 minutes then stir in the chopped tomatoes, garlic, basil and tomato purée. Season with salt and pepper then cover the pan and continue to cook for a further 20 minutes until the mixture has reduced down to a sauce-like consistency. Then stir in the chopped olives and taste to check the seasoning.

While that's happening, cook the tagliatelle in plenty of salted boiling water (with a few drops of oil added to it) for 8 minutes. Drain it thoroughly, then return it to the hot pan and toss it with the butter, half the Parmesan and all the diced Mozzarella. Season with salt and pepper, then spread the pasta in a small baking-dish, cover it with the sauce and sprinkle with the remaining Parmesan. Bake in the preheated oven for 10 minutes and serve straightaway.

Singapore noodles

For years I have searched for this recipe without success. So finally I rang Ken Lo, owner of my favourite Chinese restaurant (Memories of China in Ebury St, London), who was very happy to give me his recipe. It is, he told me, one of his own favourite dishes for one, and adds that it incorporates the Chinese principle of marrying fresh and dried ingredients.

Note: the small quantity of chicken used for this can be part of a chicken joint – where the rest is used for chicken Waldorf salad (on *page 170*).

2–3 oz rice noodles (50–75 g)
3 dried mushrooms
1 heaped dessertspoon dried shrimps
2 tablespoons oil
1 onion, chopped
1 rasher of bacon, chopped
1 clove of garlic, chopped
1 teaspoon grated fresh ginger
1 level teaspoon Madras curry powder
½ teaspoon salt
1 oz shredded cooked chicken or pork (25 g)
1 oz peeled prawns, fresh or frozen (25 g), chopped into thirds
2 spring onions, finely chopped
2 tablespoons of the mushroom soaking water
¾ tablespoon soy sauce
1 tablespoon sherry

(For notes on the Chinese ingredients, see page 20)

First of all place the shrimps and mushrooms in a jug, cover with warm water and presoak for 30 minutes. Then chop the mushrooms into small shreds. Also put the noodles in a bowlful of warm water to soak for 10–15 minutes. Meanwhile heat up the oil in a 7 inch (18 cm) frying-pan and while that's heating assemble together on a plate the shredded mushroom, onion, shrimps, chopped bacon, garlic and ginger.

When the oil is hot, throw them all in, stir well, then reduce the heat to very low and let the ingredients cook very gently for about 15 minutes (this slow cooking allows all the delicious flavours to permeate and flavour the oil).

After that add the curry powder and some salt. Then drain the noodles in a colander, shaking them well to get rid of the excess water. Now turn the heat under the pan up to medium, add the chicken and fresh prawns followed by the 2 tablespoons of mushroom water and the chopped spring onion.

Add the noodles to the pan then, using either a fork or chopsticks (!), toss the noodles around to get all the other ingredients incorporated and distributed evenly in the noodles. Finally add the soy sauce and sherry, toss everything well again, then serve straightaway by themselves – they don't need any accompaniment.

Right: Marinated kipper and potato salad, page 164; Scrambled eggs with smoked salmon, page 47.

Risotto vongole

This is a risotto made in the traditional Italian way with proper Italian rice that gives an authentic creamy texture. Vongole are tiny clams which. can be bought in 7 oz tins (200 g) from delicatessens and good food stores (that is the nett weight by the way and includes the liquor which is essential for this recipe).

Italian (arborio) rice measured to the 3 fl oz level in a glass measuring jug (75 ml)
7 oz tin of shelled clams (vongole) (200 g)
½ oz butter (10 g)
1 teaspoon olive oil
1 small onion, finely chopped
1 clove of garlic, crushed
3 fl oz white wine (75 ml)
approx 6 fl oz boiling water (175 ml)
1 dessertspoon fresh chopped parsley
salt and freshly milled black pepper

Start off by melting the butter with the oil in a medium-sized saucepan, then add the onion and cook for 5 minutes to soften. Then add the garlic and cook for a couple of minutes more before stirring in the rice to get it coated and glistening with the butter. Add a little salt then pour in the white wine and cook very gently (uncovered) until the rice has absorbed all the liquid.

Meanwhile drain the tin of clams, reserving the clam juice. When all the wine has been absorbed, pour the clam juice onto the rice, give one gentle stir then continue to cook until the rice has absorbed all the juice. After that add one ladleful of boiling water to the rice, and when that too has been absorbed, add one more ladleful until the rice is tender (you may not need all the second ladleful, but if the rice does need it add it judiciously).

When the rice is cooked, season as required with salt and pepper, then stir in the clams and fresh parsley. Now cover the pan with a clean tea-towel and leave the risotto to stand in a warm place for 5 minutes before serving.

Left: Fennel salad à la Grecque, page 166; Singapore noodles, page 128.

Chinese fried rice with prawns

For this you have to start off with cold *cooked rice – because if the rice is hot it all goes sticky on you. So prepare ahead by cooking a 2 fl oz (55 ml) measure of rice in 4 fl oz (110 ml) of water according to the method on page 134.*

cooked white rice
1 oz peeled prawns (25 g), defrosted if frozen, or 1 tablespoon Chinese dried shrimps, presoaked (*see page 20*)
1½ tablespoons peas, fresh or frozen
1 tablespoon oil
1 onion, finely chopped
1 rasher of bacon, finely chopped
1 egg, beaten
1 spring onion, split lengthways and finely chopped, including the green part
1 teaspoon soy sauce
1 extra teaspoon of oil
salt

Note: this can be varied in all kinds of ways. You could, for instance, use shredded cooked chicken instead of prawns, or vegetables (shredded mushrooms, leeks, whatever's available) could replace the meat content.

If the peas are frozen put them in a sieve and run them under the hot tap for a few seconds to defrost them, then let them drain. If you are using dried shrimps, drain them after presoaking and dry them; if fresh prawns, then they should be cut into thirds.

When you're ready to cook the fried rice, heat the oil in a 7 inch (18 cm) frying-pan, then add the onion and bacon and cook them over a high heat for about 3 minutes, then add the peas and prawns (or shrimps) and continue to cook for a further minute. Now, using a draining spoon, remove everything to a plate, leaving the oil in the pan and adding one extra teaspoonful.

Cold rice often gets stuck together, so use your hands to fluff and separate the grains, then when the oil is as hot as you dare sprinkle in the rice grains and stir-fry them in the hot oil for one minute. Then return the other ingredients and continue to stir-fry for another 30 seconds.

Season with salt then spread all the ingredients evenly over the base of the pan, and pour in the beaten egg, continuing to stir. (A warning note here: it will begin to look disastrously gungy but fear not: keep stirring and turning the mixture and the egg will soon cook, leaving no trace of stickiness but just forming itself into little bits of cooked egg.) Finally stir in the spring onion and soy sauce, give it all one good stir, then serve.

Macaroni cheese with courgettes and bacon

I like this made with the long pasta quills, sometimes called penne, *but wholewheat macaroni makes a good alternative. The courgettes can be replaced with leeks, broad beans or broccoli sprigs and, for a vegetarian, in addition to these the bacon can be replaced by mushrooms.*

2–3 oz macaroni (50–75 g)
1 tablespoon olive oil
4 oz courgettes (110 g), sliced with their skins on (not too thinly)
2 oz bacon (50 g), chopped
salt

For the sauce:

½ oz butter (10 g)
½ oz flour (10 g)
5 fl oz milk (150 ml)
1½ oz grated Cheddar cheese (40 g)
freshly grated nutmeg
1 fl oz double cream (25 ml)
salt and freshly milled black pepper

For the topping:

1 tablespoon Parmesan
1 tablespoon breadcrumbs
a pinch of cayenne
1 tomato, sliced

For this you'll need a 6 inch (15 cm) shallow gratin dish. Also preheat the grill.

Start off by bringing a panful of water to the boil, then add the macaroni together with some salt and a few drops of oil. Bring back to the boil then cook for 10 minutes.

While that's happening heat a tablespoon of olive oil in a frying-pan and, over a medium heat, cook the courgettes and chopped bacon in it to soften and colour the courgettes. At the same time, in a separate pan melt the butter for the sauce and stir in the flour, then add the milk bit by bit, stirring until you have a smooth sauce. Now leave it to cook gently for 4–5 minutes, then stir in the grated cheese, a seasoning of salt, pepper and freshly grated nutmeg, and finally the cream.

When the macaroni is ready, drain it in a colander, then return it to the hot saucepan, along with the courgettes and bacon. Pour in the sauce then stir to amalgamate everything well over a gentle heat, until it's all reheated. Then transfer the pasta mixture to the gratin dish, mix the Parmesan and breadcrumbs together, then sprinkle this all over the top. Sprinkle a pinch or so of cayenne over this, then arrange slices of tomato over the top. Place the dish under the grill for a few minutes, until the top is nicely browned.

Frying-pan paella

I have to confess that for years I avoided making a paella, ever since I read in one cookery book that one of the ingredients was a 'singing bird'. Simply on humanitarian grounds I couldn't contemplate it. However, after fourteen years of marriage, my husband pressed me to make one with rather simpler ingredients, and we are both delighted with the result.

white rice measured to the 2½ fl oz level in a measuring jug (60 ml) – you probably won't be able to get Spanish rice, so Italian is best
¼ lb fresh prawns in their shells (110 g)
½ medium-sized red pepper, chopped
1 tablespoon olive oil
1 small onion, chopped
1 large clove of garlic, finely chopped
a generous pinch of saffron
4 tomatoes, peeled and chopped
⅓ teaspoon paprika
1 oz Spanish chorizo sausage (25 g), sliced in ¼ inch (5 mm) rounds
1 oz frozen peas (25 g)
salt and freshly milled black pepper

Shell the prawns – it will take 10 minutes at the most – but leave three prawns in their shells. Cover the peeled prawns and leave them in a cool place. Now place all the shells in a saucepan, cover with ¾ pint (425 ml) of cold water, add a little salt and boil briskly for 15 minutes to make a lovely prawn-flavoured stock.

Meanwhile take a heavy 7 inch (18 cm) frying-pan and heat the oil in it, then add the pepper, onion and garlic and let them cook gently for 10 minutes. While that's happening, put the saffron into a mortar and crush it with the pestle.

When the stock is ready, strain it into a jug and discard the shells, then spoon a couple of tablespoons of stock onto the saffron to soak it a little. Next stir the rice into the frying-pan and stir it around until all the grains are coated with oil and they begin to look transparent. When that has happened pour in the chopped tomatoes and paprika, followed by 4 fl oz (110 ml) of the stock plus the saffron liquid. Sprinkle in ½ teaspoon of salt, stir once then leave the pan on a very low heat to barely simmer for 15 minutes, shaking the pan from time to time to prevent sticking (you do have to stay with it and keep an eye on it).

After 15 minutes most of the liquid will have been absorbed. Now add the chorizo but *don't* stir or the rice will break and go sticky. Just push the pieces in with a skewer. Now add another 4 fl oz (110 ml) of stock and let it simmer as before just shaking the pan now and then.

Meanwhile measure out the peas and rinse them under a hot running tap for a minute to defrost them. Now sprinkle the peas and the peeled prawns, plus the prawns still in their shells, over the surface of the paella. Add one more fluid ounce of stock and carry on cooking for a further 5–10 minutes for the prawns and peas to heat through (still shaking the pan from time to time). You can turn the heat up a bit at this stage to accelerate the process – but no stirring! As soon as they are hot, you can incorporate them gently into the rest of the ingredients.

Then serve the paella on a warmed, deep soup plate and drink some chilled Spanish white wine with it.

Note: the above is obviously a simplified version as it had to be scaled down for one, but if you would like to use 2 oz (50 g) of chopped chicken breast and cut the prawns by 2 oz (50 g) that would be OK.

Basic rice

Many of the recipes in this book are best served with rice and since so many people seem to be apprehensive about cooking rice (quite unnecessarily, I might add) I thought I would include directions for cooking one portion of rice, and a couple of variations. Follow these instructions and you'll have perfect rice every time.

long-grain rice, measured to the 2½ fl oz (60 ml) level in a glass measuring jug
5 fl oz boiling water (150 ml)
1 teaspoon oil
salt

Heat the oil in a small, solid-based saucepan then add the rice and, using a wooden spoon, stir the grains around to get them well coated and glistening. Now add the boiling water and half a teaspoon of salt, stir just once as the liquid comes up to simmering point, then cover the pan with a tight-fitting lid. Turn the heat down to the gentlest simmer, then leave it completely alone for 15 minutes. Before then don't stir it or even peer at it.

After 15 minutes test a few grains and check to see that there is no liquid left in the pan when you tilt it sideways. If it has all been absorbed, the rice is cooked. Tip it out onto a serving dish and lightly fluff the grains up with a skewer. If you need to keep it warm, for up to 10 minutes, cover the bowl with a clean tea-cloth (which will absorb the steam and help keep the grains separate) and place over a pan of barely simmering water.

Note: if you are using *brown rice*, then leave it to cook for 40 minutes before taking off the lid and testing it. Also for *onion rice*, sweat a teaspoon of chopped onion in the oil for 2 minutes before stirring in the rice.

Spiced rice

This is a variation on the last recipe, which is just right for serving with curries, kebabs or other spiced dishes.

long-grain rice, measured to the 2½ fl oz level in a glass measuring jug (60 ml)
5 fl oz boiling water (150 ml)
½ oz butter (10 g)
1 teaspoon oil
½ small onion, finely chopped
½ inch piece of cinnamon stick (1 cm)
¼ teaspoon cumin seeds, crushed
1 cardamom pod, crushed
1 teaspoon ground turmeric
1 bayleaf
salt

Melt the butter with the oil in a small thick-based saucepan then soften the onion in it for about 3 minutes. After that stir in the spices, bayleaf and salt and cook for a minute or so for the heat to draw out the fragrance.

Then add the rice and stir it around to get it coated with the oil and spices, and pour in the boiling water. Stir once, cover with a tight-fitting lid, then simmer at the gentlest possible simmer for 15 minutes or until the rice is tender. When cooked, lift out the cinnamon and bayleaf (which will obligingly have come to the surface), then tip the rice into a warmed serving dish and fluff up with a skewer.

Pilaff rice

Yet another variation on the same theme, this one with something of a Middle Eastern flavour to it. Pine kernels, by the way, are available from delicatessens.

long-grain rice, measured to the 2½ fl oz level in a glass measuring jug (60 ml)
5 fl oz boiling water (150 ml)
1 dessertspoon oil
½ small onion, chopped
½ oz pine kernels (10 g)
½ teaspoon currants
½ inch stick of cinnamon (1 cm)
salt

Heat the oil in a small thick-based saucepan and soften the onion in it for 5 minutes before sprinkling in the pine kernels and cooking them for just one minute. Then add the currants and the cinnamon, and stir in the rice to get it nicely coated with the oil.

Pour in the boiling water, season with salt, then put a lid on the pan and cook at the gentlest possible simmer for 15 minutes or until all the water has been absorbed and the grains are tender. Before serving remove the cinnamon and use a skewer to fluff up the rice and distribute the pine kernels and other ingredients evenly.

The Lone Vegetarian

Spiced winter vegetables in yoghurt

Cauliflower casserole with Provençale topping

Mushroom curry

Deep-fried gnocchi with tomato sauce

Cheese, sage and onion sausages

Florentine eggs

Gratinée of eggs Basque

Petit courgette soufflé

Sri Lankan egg curry

Vegetarian moussaka

Gougère with leeks and Mornay sauce

Sautéed spiced vegetables with lentils

Fried Mozzarella with Provençale sauce

One is fun!

Ever since I first started writing about cookery and demonstrating the subject on television I have always made a point of including a high percentage of recipes for vegetarians. This is partly because I happen to enjoy vegetarian food very much myself, but it is also because I thought we should eat less meat – and that was long before meat became a controversial health issue. Intensive rearing, requiring ten pounds of grain to produce one pound of meat, always seemed quite wrong. In my ideal world animals would be reared and grazed naturally – obviously I would have to pay more for my meat, but I would cheerfully eat less of it.

But enough of meat – because what I have tried to do is to cross the great divide between vegetarians and meat-eaters. Vegetarian recipes *ought* to be better integrated into cooking as a whole, not something set apart from the mainstream. While I appreciate how irritating it must be for a vegetarian to find the odd anchovy or bacon rasher in an otherwise suitable recipe, it is equally frustrating for a meat-eater wanting to use a vegetarian recipe to come across some strange esoteric ingredient he has never heard of. There are none of those in the recipes that follow, I promise.

Spiced winter vegetables in yoghurt

There comes a time in every winter when I feel I want to jazz up the vegetables that are available. In fact this recipe does more than that – it makes a delicious vegetarian meal that needs nothing more than some crispy bread and butter to go with it.

½ small cauliflower (6 oz, 175 g), separated into small florets
1 medium carrot quartered lengthways and cut thinly across
2 oz onion (50 g), chopped
½ small cooking apple, cored and diced
1 tablespoon oil
¼ teaspoon cumin seeds
¼ teaspoon coriander seeds
¼ teaspoon mustard seeds
¼ teaspoon turmeric
a pinch of cayenne
2 large tablespoons natural yoghurt
salt and freshly milled black pepper

For the garnish: 1 dessertspoon fresh chopped parsley

Start off by crushing the cumin, coriander and mustard seeds, either with a pestle and mortar or by using the end of a rolling-pin and a basin. Then heat the oil in a medium saucepan and stir the prepared vegetables and apple into it. Cook them over a fairly high heat until they're lightly browned, stirring now and then.

After that turn the heat down low and stir in the crushed seeds, turmeric, cayenne, a seasoning of salt and pepper, and finally the yoghurt. Bring it all up to simmering point, then cover the pan and cook for 15 minutes or so, or until the vegetables are just tender. To finish off, uncover the pan, increase the heat and cook for a few minutes more to reduce the juices to a good sauce-like consistency.

Cauliflower casserole with Provençale topping

This takes its name from the crisp cheese, herb and bread-crumb crust which forms a topping and makes this look so bright and colourful. It's also lightning quick to make.

6 oz cauliflower florets (175 g)
8 oz (225 g) red ripe tomatoes, peeled and chopped
¼ red or green pepper, chopped
1 medium courgette, sliced
1 medium onion, chopped
1 tablespoon oil
½ large clove of garlic, crushed
½ teaspoon crushed coriander seeds
⅓ teaspoon oregano
salt and freshly milled black pepper

For the topping:

the other half of the clove of garlic, crushed
few sprigs of parsley, approx 1 handful
1 oz wholewheat bread (25 g)
1 teaspoon of fresh herbs or 1 finely chopped spring onion
1½ oz grated cheese (40 g), Cheddar or Parmesan
salt and freshly milled black pepper

Start by heating the oil in a medium-sized saucepan, then soften the onion, garlic and pepper in it for 5 minutes. After that add the courgette together with the coriander and oregano, and let these cook for a further 5 minutes. Now pour in the tomatoes, season with salt and pepper, bring up to a simmer then add the cauliflower florets (arranging them in an upright position so that the stalk ends cook in the sauce and the flowery ends in the steam).

Put a lid on and simmer for about 12–15 minutes or until the cauliflower is just tender but still retains some bite. Meanwhile preheat the grill. And while that's happening place all the topping ingredients, except the cheese, in the goblet of a liquidiser and blend them together for a few seconds to form bright green crumbs – then mix the crumbs with the cheese.

When the cauliflower is ready spoon it into a gratin dish, pour the sauce all over it, then top with the cheese-crumb mixture. Flash it under the grill, fairly close to the heat, for a minute or two until the breadcrumbs are crusty and browned. Serve straightaway. This would go well with brown rice if you're extra hungry.

Mushroom curry

This is a light, fresh-tasting curry, for which I suggest you use the dark, more open-gilled mushrooms for a better flavour.

6 oz mushrooms (175 g), sliced
1 medium-sized potato, cut into small dice
1 small tin of Italian tomatoes or 3 ripe tomatoes, skinned and chopped
1 small onion, chopped
½ oz butter (10 g)
1 tablespoon oil
1 small clove of garlic, crushed
1 teaspoon grated root ginger
½ teaspoon turmeric
1 level teaspoon Madras curry powder
1 tablespoon natural yoghurt
1 teaspoon lemon juice
salt and freshly milled black pepper

In a small flameproof casserole melt the butter together with the oil. Then dry the potato dice as much as possible in a clean tea-towel and add them to the casserole together with the chopped onion. Stir them around then cook over a medium heat for 5 minutes before adding the garlic, ginger, turmeric and curry powder. Cook for another minute then stir in the mushrooms, making sure they get a good spicy coating.

After a couple of minutes' more cooking, stir in the yoghurt and lemon juice and, finally, the chopped tomatoes. Season with salt and pepper, give it all one last stir, then cover the casserole and cook over a gentle heat for 20–25 minutes or until the potatoes are quite tender (stir it around from time to time to prevent it sticking).

Five minutes before the end of the cooking time, take the lid off and, if there is rather a lot of liquid, continue to cook uncovered so that it can reduce down a little. Serve on a bed of rice.

Deep-fried gnocchi with tomato sauce

I particularly like this way of cooking these little Italian cheese-and-semolina savouries. The deep-frying gives them a lovely crisp coating, and the pungent concentrated sauce is evocative of so many sunny Italian days!

1 oz semolina (25 g)
1 large egg
3 fl oz milk (75 ml)
1 oz freshly grated Parmesan (25 g)
1 oz Mozzarella cheese (25 g), finely diced
2 tablespoons dry white breadcrumbs
seasoned flour
freshly grated nutmeg
oil for deep-frying
salt and freshly milled black pepper

For the tomato sauce:

6 oz ripe tomatoes, skinned and chopped, or use tinned chopped Italian tomatoes
1 tablespoon oil
2 oz chopped onion (50 g)
1 small clove of garlic, crushed
½ level teaspooon dried basil
salt and freshly milled black pepper

Begin by making up the tomato sauce first. Heat one tablespoon of oil in a small saucepan and soften the onion and garlic in it for 5 minutes or so before adding the tomatoes and basil. Season with salt and pepper, give it a good stir, then cook (uncovered) for half an hour over a fairly gentle heat to reduce the mixture by at least half. Keep an eye on it to make sure it doesn't stick to the bottom of the pan.

Meanwhile heat the milk in a pan with a pinch of salt, some pepper and nutmeg stirred in. When it comes to the boil, shoot the semolina into the milk and stir over the heat until the mixture is thick enough to stand a spoon up in. Then take the pan off the heat.

Now beat the egg well and pour half of it into a shallow dish (and keep this on one side). Add the Parmesan, Mozzarella and the rest of the beaten egg to the semolina mixture, beat it well until the cheese has melted, then taste to check the seasoning. Next lightly oil a baking-sheet and with the help of a spatula (slightly dampened) spread the mixture out evenly onto it, shaping it into a square about ½ inch (1 cm) thick.

Leave the mixture to cool and firm up, then cut it into diamond-shaped pieces. Use the spatula to ease each one off, dust them first with seasoned flour, then dip them into the reserved beaten eggs and finally in the breadcrumbs to coat them well.

Heat a pan filled up to one-third with oil till it reaches 360°F (185°C) or, if you haven't got a cooking thermometer, to the point where a small cube of bread thrown in will brown in one minute. Deep-fry the gnocchi until they are golden-brown – you may need to do this in two batches if you want to keep them separate. Serve them with the tomato sauce, re-heated, if necessary.

Cheese, sage and onion sausages

The problem with this recipe, I think, is how to make it sound appealing because it tastes so much better than the title might lead you to believe. If you trust me, I think you'll be pleasantly surprised.

2 oz freshly made wholewheat breadcrumbs (50 g)

1½ oz strong Cheddar cheese (40 g), grated

2 spring onions, finely chopped, including the green parts

⅓ teaspoon dried sage

½ teaspoon mustard powder

1 large egg yolk

salt and freshly milled black pepper

For the coating and frying:

1 egg white

1½ tablespoons fresh breadcrumbs

1 tablespoon Parmesan cheese

groundnut oil

In a mixing bowl, mix together the 2 oz of breadcrumbs, the cheese, spring onion, sage and mustard powder and a seasoning of salt and pepper. Then add the egg yolk and, using a fork, stir to bind the mixture together.

Now pour enough oil in to cover the base of a 7 inch (18 cm) frying-pan (about 1–1½ tablespoons) and place the pan on the heat. Now mix the 1½ tablespoons of breadcrumbs (for the coating) with the Parmesan in a bowl, then in another bowl beat the egg white to the soft-peak stage.

Next divide the sausage mixture into four and roll each portion into a sausage-shape, using your hands. Then dip each one, first into the egg white and then into the breadcrumbs and cheese mixture to give an even coating. Then fry in hot oil till crisp and golden on all sides. Drain on crumpled kitchen paper and serve with fresh tomato sauce (*see page 142*) and a crisp green vegetable.

Florentine eggs

This favourite classic egg dish is usually either baked in the oven or else the eggs are poached separately and served with a spinach and cheese sauce. For one person I've adapted it so that everything goes into a heated gratin dish and is cooked under the grill.

2 large eggs, or 1 or 3, depending on your appetite
6 oz frozen spinach (175 g)
1 teaspoon butter
½ oz butter (10 g)
1 rounded dessertspoon flour (½ oz, 10 g)
8 fl oz milk (225 ml)
freshly grated nutmeg
1 tablespoon cream
1½ oz grated cheese (40 g), I like to use strong Cheddar for this
salt and freshly milled black pepper

You also need a 9 inch (23 cm) gratin dish, buttered

First put the frozen spinach into a saucepan together with a teaspoon of butter and some salt and pepper over a medium heat, then allow it to defrost and collapse into the butter (this takes about 10 minutes if it's frozen solid).

Meanwhile put the ½ oz (10 g) of butter, the flour and the milk into a small saucepan then, using a balloon whisk, whisk these together over a medium heat until the sauce has thickened and come to the boil. Season it with salt, pepper and a generous grating of nutmeg, and let it simmer very gently for 5 minutes, then stir in the cream.

While that's happening, preheat the grill. Then arrange the hot spinach over the base of the gratin dish, leaving two oval spaces for the eggs (or however many you are using). Then break the eggs into these spaces, season them with salt and pepper, then quickly pour the sauce evenly over the spinach and eggs. Now finish off by sprinkling the grated cheese all over, and grill them – about 4 inches (10 cm) away from the heat – for 12–14 minutes depending on how you like your eggs (you can always lift the cheese up a little and have a peek at the eggs and return them to the grill if they're not done enough for you). This needs lots of crusty wholewheat bread to go with it.

Gratinée of eggs Basque

An ingenious little supper dish for one, this, but with plenty of colour and flavour. If you're less hungry, just use one egg.

2 large eggs
1 medium-sized courgette, sliced thinly
½ small green pepper, chopped into ½ inch (1 cm) squares
½ medium onion, chopped small
2 red ripe tomatoes or 2 tablespoons of Italian tinned tomatoes
1 tablespoon olive oil
1 small clove of garlic, crushed
1½ oz grated cheese, any variety (40 g)
1 teaspoon fresh chopped parsley
salt and freshly milled black pepper

1 round 6 inch (15 cm) Apilco gratin dish, buttered

Preheat the grill, pour boiling water over the tomatoes (if you're using fresh ones), then after a couple of minutes peel off the skins and chop the flesh up roughly.

Now in a 7 inch (18 cm) thick-based frying-pan heat the oil and fry the onion and pepper over a medium heat for about 10 minutes until golden and almost cooked. Then draw them to one side of the pan and add the courgette slices: brown these on both sides, then add the garlic and stir everything together.

Next add the chopped tomatoes and a good seasoning of salt and pepper, and let it all cook for 1 minute more. Now spoon the mixture into a gratin dish and spread it out evenly, making two little spaces for the eggs. Break 2 eggs into these spaces, season them, then sprinkle the cheese all over. Place the dish approximately 4 inches (10 cm) away from the grill, and cook for 10–15 minutes, depending on how you like your eggs. Serve sprinkled with chopped parsley and with lots of crusty French bread.

Petit courgette soufflé

A soufflé actually works better for one than if made for a larger number of people. This one – light and delicate – goes well with a tomato salad and some French bread.

6 oz courgettes (175 g)
1 large egg, separated, *plus* 1 extra egg white
1½ oz butter (40 g)
1 rounded dessertspoon flour
2 fl oz milk (55 ml)
1 dessertspoon finely chopped parsley
1 dessertspoon finely chopped chives or spring onion
½ oz grated cheese, Gruyère or Cheddar (10 g)
freshly grated nutmeg
a pinch of cayenne
1 dessertspoon grated Parmesan
salt and freshly milled black pepper

Preheat the oven to gas mark 6, 400°F, 200°C
You'll also need a 5 inch (13 cm) diameter soufflé dish (well buttered) and a small roasting tin filled with 1 inch (2·5 cm) of hot water placed in the oven while it's preheating

First cut the courgettes into four lengthways then slice them thinly. Next melt the butter in a medium-sized saucepan and cook the courgette pieces gently in it, seasoning them with salt and pepper then putting a lid on the pan so that they cook in their own juice – they'll need about 8 minutes and you should give them a stir every now and then to prevent them sticking.

When they're ready, stir in the flour to soak up all the buttery juices, then gradually add the milk bit by bit, stirring until you have a smooth mixture. Now remove the pan from the heat and stir in the egg yolk, parsley, chives, grated cheese, a good grating of nutmeg and a pinch of cayenne. Taste to check the seasoning, then transfer the mixture to a mixing bowl.

In another large, roomy bowl whisk the egg whites to the soft-peak stage (don't over-beat or they will start to go floppy), then carefully fold them – about a third of the mixture at a time – into the courgette mixture. Finally pile the whole lot into the soufflé dish, sprinkle the Parmesan cheese on top and place the dish in the roasting tin containing the hot water, and bake the soufflé for 30–35 minutes.

Sri Lankan egg curry

2 eggs
½ oz butter (10 g)
1 dessertspoon oil
1 small onion, chopped
1 small carrot, sliced into very thin rounds
½ small green pepper, chopped into small dice
3 inch stick of celery (7·5 cm), cut into matchstick strips about 2 inches long (5 cm)
1 small clove of garlic, crushed
1 teaspoon grated root ginger
½ teaspoon turmeric
1 heaped teaspoon Madras curry powder
1 level dessertspoon plain flour
½ pint hot water (275 ml)
1 oz grated creamed coconut (25 g)
lemon juice
salt and freshly milled black pepper

This curry borrows the Sri Lankan idea of using coconut to thicken and flavour it. You need to use creamed coconut, which is unsweetened and contains all the natural coconut oil. It's available at most supermarkets.

The eggs need to be hardboiled, so cover them with cold water in a small saucepan, then bring them up to the boil and give them 7 minutes from then. Next take them off the heat and run them under cold water to cool them.

Meanwhile heat the butter and oil in a small casserole or frying-pan with a lid, then add the prepared onion, carrot, pepper and celery and stir them around to get them nicely coated. Cook for 5 minutes before adding the garlic and ginger and continue to cook for another couple of minutes. Then stir in the turmeric, curry powder and flour and stir to soak up the juice. Now gradually add the hot water, stirring after each addition to make a smooth sauce. Season with salt and pepper, then stir in the creamed coconut. Cover the pan and simmer the vegetables gently for 10 minutes or until they are all tender. Then taste to check the seasoning and add a tiny bit of lemon juice to sharpen it.

Finally peel the hardboiled eggs, slice them in half lengthways, then arrange them in the curry making sure they are covered by the sauce. Simmer for just a minute more to heat them through, then serve with rice and chutney.

Vegetarian moussaka

*There is 1 oz (25 g) of lentils in this recipe, which is a very small amount to cook in one go. So I suggest you treat this as a Mixed Double by cooking 2 oz (50 g) of lentils and use the other half the next day for either sautéed spiced vegetables with lentils (*see page 152*) or lentil and mushroom salad with green peppercorns (*see page 167*).*

1 oz whole green or brown lentils (25 g)
2 fl oz water (55 ml)
½ small aubergine (3 oz, 75 g), chopped into small cubes
2 tablespoons oil
1 small onion, finely chopped
2 oz green pepper (50 g), chopped small
1 clove of garlic, crushed
2 tablespoons red wine or dry cider
1 dessertspoon tomato purée
⅛ teaspoon ground cinnamon
1 teaspoon chopped parsley
salt and freshly milled black pepper

For the topping:

1 egg
2 tablespoons natural yoghurt
1 tablespoon grated Parmesan cheese
freshly grated nutmeg

Preheat the oven to gas mark 4, 350°F, 180°C

First of all cook the lentils in the water (no salt added) at a gentle simmer for about 30 minutes or until they are softened and all the water has been absorbed. (If you are cooking a double quantity – see above – measure out half of them into a bowl and when they have got quite cold, cover the bowl with clingfilm and store in the fridge.)

Next prepare the aubergines: place the cubes in a colander, sprinkle them with a little salt, then cover with a plate weighted down with a saucer topped with some scale-weights. Leave them to drain for 20 minutes, then squeeze them dry in a clean tea-cloth. Meanwhile heat 1 tablespoon of oil in a frying-pan and cook the onion and pepper together in it until they are softened – about 8–10 minutes. Then remove them to a plate, add the rest of the oil to the pan and cook the aubergine, which will also take about 10 minutes to soften.

After that add the garlic, cook that for a minute then return the onion and pepper to the pan. Now mix the wine and tomato purée together with the cinnamon and parsley in a jug, then pour this into the vegetable mixture. Stir in the softened lentils, add a good seasoning of salt and pepper, then mix until everything is thoroughly combined. Next spoon the whole lot into a 5 inch (13 cm) ramekin dish.

Beat the egg together with the yoghurt, Parmesan and a little freshly grated nutmeg, and finally pour this over the top of the vegetables. Bake in the oven for 30 minutes or until the top is puffy and golden. Brown rice or wholewheat pitta bread would be a nice accompaniment.

Gougère with leeks and Mornay sauce

A gougère is a baked ring of choux paste which is light and crisp on the outside but creamy and puffy within. So often people think that choux pastry is only for experts but if you follow the recipe exactly you'll discover it is really the easiest pastry of all to make. This one has some buttered leeks cooked in it, then it is all coated with a light sauce.

For the filling:

1 leek (approx 2½ oz, 60 g, after cleaning and trimming), chopped into ½ inch (1 cm) pieces

½ oz butter (10 g)

For the paste:

1½ oz strong plain flour (40 g)

1 oz butter (25 g)

2½ fl oz water (60 ml)

1 egg

1 oz Gruyère cheese (25 g), grated

¼ teaspoon ground mace or nutmeg

salt and freshly milled black pepper

For the sauce:

½ oz butter (10 g)

4 fl oz milk (110 ml)

1 heaped teaspoon flour

½ oz Gruyère cheese (10 g), grated

1 dessertspoon finely chopped spring onion or fresh snipped chives

salt and freshly milled black pepper

Preheat the oven to gas mark 6, 400°F, 200°C

First soften the leek by melting the butter in a small saucepan, then adding the pieces of leek and covering the pan. Now leave the leek to sweat over a gentle heat for 10–15 minutes.

Meanwhile you can be making up the choux paste. Cut the butter up into small pieces then place them in another small pan together with the water, then place the pan over a moderate heat and stir with a wooden spoon. You are going to need to shoot the flour quickly into the water when the butter has melted, so have it sifted ready on a sheet of greaseproof paper that has been folded once and then opened out again.

When the butter has melted and the mixture come to the boil, turn off the heat and tip the flour all in one go into the pan with one hand, while you beat the mixture briskly with the other (with a wooden spoon or, better still, an electric hand-whisk). Beat until you have a smooth ball of paste that has left the sides of the saucepan clean, then beat the egg in, a little at a time – until you have a smooth glossy paste. Finally lift the sweated leek from its pan with a draining spoon, and stir this into the paste until well incorporated, followed by the grated Gruyère, the mace (or nutmeg) and salt and pepper.

At this point grease a baking-sheet lightly, then hold it under cold running water for a moment and tap it sharply to get rid of the excess moisture (this will help create a steamy atmosphere that helps the pastry to rise). Now spoon dessertspoonfuls of the paste onto the sheet so that they touch each other and form a circle. Then bake in the oven for 10 minutes, and after that increase the heat to gas mark 7, 425°F, 220°C and cook for a further 20–25 minutes.

While the gougère is cooking, make up the sauce. Place the butter, milk and flour in a small saucepan and whisk it all together over a medium heat until the sauce is smooth and lump-free. Then cook it very gently for 5 minutes, and just before serving, stir in the grated cheese and spring onion (or chives). Taste and season as required, then pour this over the gougère before serving to give a thin coating all over.

Sautéed spiced vegetables with lentils

This is a colourful, made-in-moments recipe and if you serve it with some brown rice it's also very filling. I would suggest – since cooking just 1 oz (25 g) of lentils is hard to justify – that you make this part of a Mixed Double. Cook 2 oz (50 g) of lentils then store half of them and use the next day in the delicious lentil and mushroom salad with green peppercorns on page 167.

1 oz lentils (25 g) cooked gently in 2 fl oz water (55 ml) for 30 minutes
1 small onion, roughly chopped
1½ oz green or red pepper (40 g), cut into small ½ inch (1 cm) strips
1 clove of garlic, crushed
1½ oz mushrooms (40 g), sliced
1 small carrot (1 oz, 25 g), sliced
6 oz skinned, chopped tomatoes (175 g)
1 tablespoon oil
1 dessertspoon yoghurt
salt and freshly milled black pepper

For the spices:

1 cardamom pod
¼ teaspoon cumin seeds
¼ teaspoon coriander seeds
⅛–¼ teaspoon of crushed dried chilli or chilli powder (depending on how hot you like it)
¼ teaspoon grated fresh root ginger

First of all put all the spices (except the ginger) into an empty frying-pan then, over a medium heat, warm them through to draw out their flavour – the aroma will tell you when this is happening. Then scrape them all into a mortar and crush them to a powder.

Now add the oil to the pan and when it's hot add the onion and pepper together with the garlic and ginger. Let these cook together for 5 minutes. After that stir in the mushroom and carrot along with the rest of the spices and continue to cook for a further 5 minutes. Then add the lentils and tomatoes, and stir well to break up the tomatoes and mix everything together.

Season well with salt and pepper, then cover the pan and let the whole lot simmer gently for 10 minutes. After that remove the lid and let the sauce bubble and reduce for a further 3–5 minutes. Then stir in the yoghurt, let it warm through, then serve straightaway.

Fried Mozzarella with Provençale sauce

4 oz Mozzarella cheese (110 g)
seasoned flour
1 small egg, beaten
3 tablespoons breadcrumbs
oil for frying

For the Provençale sauce:

4 ripe red tomatoes, skinned and chopped, or 4 heaped tablespoons of tinned chopped Italian tomatoes
½ small onion, chopped
¼ medium green pepper, chopped
1 clove of garlic, crushed
1 tablespoon olive oil
½ teaspoon dried basil
salt and freshly milled black pepper

For this interesting recipe you will need approximately half a Mozzarella (fresh if you can get it, or else use the Danish variety that is available in many shops now). You could, therefore, regard this as part of a Mixed Double with the green tagliatelle with three cheeses (page 121), to make use of the rest.

Start off by making the sauce. Heat the oil in a small saucepan then add the chopped onion and pepper, and cook them together for 5 minutes to soften. Then add the garlic, chopped tomatoes and basil, stir to break up the tomatoes a bit, and season with salt and pepper. Cook the sauce gently (uncovered) for about 15 minutes or until it has reduced and concentrated.

While that's happening, heat about 1 inch (2·5 cm) of oil in a saucepan or frying-pan until it reaches 375°F (190°C), if you have a thermometer; if not, test it by popping in a small cube of bread. If it browns in one minute the oil is ready. Now slice the Mozzarella into ¼ inch (5 mm) strips, then coat these thoroughly in the seasoned flour, trying not to leave any gaps because the cheese will ooze out while frying otherwise.

Next dip each coated slice in beaten egg to cover it, then cover each one with breadcrumbs (once again make sure it's well coated so as to seal it). When the oil is hot enough, lower the cheese slices into it and cook for 1–2 minutes or until the underside is nicely browned. Then turn them over and continue to cook until the other side has browned. Drain them on crumpled greaseproof paper then serve straightaway with the Provençale sauce.

Singular Salads and Sauces

One is fun!

One thing all nutritionists seem to agree on is that raw vegetables and salads are good for us – because even the most careful cooking can rob vegetables of some of their nutrients, and therefore eating them raw means we are getting the best from them.

In the summer months there is no problem about raw fresh salads: our homegrown (as opposed to imported) salad vegetables are crisp and full of flavour, and salads then can be kept simple. In fact it's hard to beat a plateful of skinned sliced tomatoes, sprinkled with crushed rock salt, freshly milled pepper and a few drops of fruity olive oil. And what is nicer than a few crisp lettuce leaves on their own tossed in a well flavoured vinaigrette?

What I have tried to concentrate on in this chapter are salad ideas for the leaner winter months – which can, with a little imagination, be just as prolific. Most of the salads here (with the exception of the Chinese beansprout salad) will serve one person as the main part of a meal, followed perhaps by some cheese or fruit. On the other hand, if you prefer, many of them can be used as a side-salad to accompany two separate meals. Those suitable for this would be: broad bean, raw vegetable, leek, chicory, spiced pasta, brown rice with raw vegetables and fennel salads – all of them will keep perfectly well, covered with clingfilm in the fridge, to serve again the next day.

Obviously making salads for one involves small amounts of quite a few ingredients, so you're bound to have quantities of salad vegetables left over: most of them however can be stored in the fridge for several days in tied polythene bags with a couple of air-holes in them.

Just a word about dressings: the quality of the ingredients you buy for these really is important. Pick a good fruity olive oil (I use Italian) and a good quality wine vinegar – *never* use malt vinegar. Maldon rock salt has a better salty flavour than ordinary table salt and, personally, I prefer Colman's mustard powder to any of the made-up French varieties: it gives that pure, sharp mustard flavour unadulterated by other ingredients. Anyone who likes to cook should always have lemons handy and, again, if you find yourself only using a half or a quarter of one, the rest will keep for several days in the fridge, wrapped in clingfilm.

Finally I have included a recipe for homemade mayonnaise, because I honestly believe it is best. However for sheer convenience I keep a jar of Hellman's Mayonnaise in the larder. It is useful for salad dressings and, I believe, is the best on the market.

Broad bean and salami salad

In this salad the broad beans are dressed in oil, lemon and garlic whilst still warm – this way the flavour of the dressing really permeates them as they cool. In winter 4 oz (110 g) of frozen broad beans can be used.

1 lb broad beans (450 g), weighed before shelling
1 oz salami (25 g), finely chopped
2 spring onions, finely chopped
1 teaspoon fresh chopped herbs (parsley, tarragon, chives)

For the dressing:

6 whole black peppercorns, coarsely crushed
¼ level teaspoon rock salt
½ clove of garlic, crushed
1 dessertspoon lemon juice
2 dessertspoons oil
½ teaspoon mustard powder

Make the dressing first of all. For this you need to crush the peppercorns with a pestle and mortar (or alternatively use the end of a rolling-pin and a small basin), then crush the salt together with the garlic and work them to a paste. Stir the lemon juice, oil and mustard powder into this paste then transfer the whole lot to a small screwtop jar and shake vigorously to get everything thoroughly amalgamated.

Next cook the shelled beans by placing them in a saucepan with a little salt, barely cover them with boiling water from the kettle, cover and simmer for 3–5 minutes (it's important not to overcook them or their delicate green colour will begin to turn to a khaki grey). Drain them quickly, place them in a bowl, give the dressing a good shake and pour it over the beans. Toss them around to get them nicely coated, then leave them to cool. Toss in the spring onions, herbs and salami, then serve the salad on a bed of crisp lettuce leaves.

Note: vegetarians can omit the salami and add ½ teaspoon of grated lemon rind to the dressing for a more lemony flavour.

Raw vegetable salad with yoghurt dressing

Personally I like this made with fairly finely shredded Chinese leaves, but any kind of cabbage will do (white, green or red). For a more substantial and nutritious salad a vegetarian could add 1 oz (25 g) of chopped nuts to this.

1½ oz shredded cabbage (40 g)
2 spring onions, chopped small
1 oz celery chopped small (25 g), equivalent to half a medium stalk
1 oz carrot (25 g), equivalent to half a medium carrot
½ Cox's or other dessert apple

For the dressing:

6 whole peppercorns
⅓ teaspoon rock salt
⅓ teaspoon coriander seeds
½ teaspoon mustard powder
1 dessertspoon wine vinegar
2 dessertspoons olive oil
1 heaped dessertspoon natural yoghurt

For the garnish: fresh chopped parsley
1 dessertspoon chopped walnuts

Put the shredded cabbage, spring onions and celery in a salad bowl. Then coarsely grate the carrot and the apple (leaving the skin on), and add them to the rest of the vegetables.

Now make up the dressing as follows: first crush the peppercorns and salt (either with pestle and mortar, or using the end of a rolling-pin and basin). Put the coriander seeds in a small saucepan and place the pan on a gentle heat on top of the stove. If you allow the heat to get at them while you crush them, it draws out the lovely flavour and aroma – it will only take about one minute.

Now add the coriander to the salt and peppercorns, add the mustard, then stir in first the vinegar, then the oil and then the yoghurt. Beat the mixture with a fork to get it thoroughly blended, then pour it over the vegetables and toss them well to get them all evenly coated with the dressing. Now the salad is ready and all it needs is a sprinkling of parsley and chopped nuts.

Leeks à la Grecque

While this is, more properly, a salad-type dish and should be chilled while the leeks absorb the flavour of the sauce, it is possible to serve it straightaway, hot, as an accompaniment.

2 slim leeks, trimmed
1 medium carrot, peeled
1 stick of celery, washed
1 fl oz olive oil (25 ml)
1 fl oz dry white wine (25 ml)
2 oz chopped onion (50 g)
½ level teaspoon oregano
1 bayleaf
1 small clove of garlic, crushed
2 rounded teaspoons tomato purée
2 teaspoons lemon juice
salt and freshly milled black pepper

To wash the leeks, make a small incision in the top of each leek and fan the top layers under cold water to remove any dust and grit. Then cut the carrot and celery into thin matchstick strips no more than ¼ inch (5 mm) wide, place them in a saucepan and cover with boiling water.

Next arrange the whole leeks in a steamer and place that over the pan containing the carrot and celery, and cover the steamer with a lid. (An alternative, if you haven't got a steamer, would be to use a small colander with a saucepan lid on top.) Boil the celery and carrots for 10 minutes or until they are cooked and the leeks are steamed till just tender.

After that drain the vegetables and reserve the cooking water. Arrange the leeks in a serving dish with the other vegetables on top. Measure 3 fl oz (75 ml) of the cooking water and return this to the pan along with the oil, wine, onion, oregano, bayleaf and garlic.

Bring to the boil and simmer very gently (uncovered) for 20 minutes. Then stir in the tomato purée, lemon juice and a good seasoning of salt and pepper. Finally pour the hot sauce over the vegetables and chill until ready to serve.

Chicory, orange and walnut salad

This salad has a wonderfully crunchy texture, and the orange helps to make it most attractive to look at. Oh yes, it also tastes delicious.

2 small heads of chicory
2 oz celery (50 g), finely chopped
3 spring onions, finely chopped, including the green parts
1 oz walnuts (25 g), roughly chopped
4 orange segments, or 6 if they are small

For the dressing:

1 small clove of garlic
½ teaspoon mustard powder
½ teaspoon salt
1 teaspoon wine vinegar
3 teaspoons oil
2 teaspoons single cream
freshly milled black pepper

Prepare the chicory by simply slicing each head across into ¼ inch (5 mm) slices, discard any stalky bits, then place the rest in a salad bowl together with the celery, spring onion and chopped walnuts. Now, using a sharp paring knife, cut off the outer pith from the orange segments and remove any pips, then cut each segment across into four and add these to the salad.

Now to make the dressing: crush the garlic together with the mustard, salt and pepper, then add this paste to a screwtop jar. Pour in the wine vinegar, followed by the oil, then put the lid on the jar and shake vigorously to mix everything. Next add the cream, cover the jar and shake again to incorporate the cream. Then pour the dressing over the salad, and toss all the ingredients around in it so they get a thorough coating.

Right: Gratinée of eggs Basque, (top), page 146; Potatoes Niçoise, (bottom), page 180.

Spiced wholewheat pasta salad

Here's a very quick supper dish that would suit a vegetarian well. Or it would provide an excellent side-salad for a couple of days – especially good with cold chicken.

1 egg
2 oz wholewheat macaroni (50 g)
1 oz green pepper (25 g), finely chopped
2 spring onions, finely chopped
¼ dessert apple, chopped small
drops of oil
salt

For the dressing:

½ clove of garlic, crushed
⅓ teaspoon salt
⅓ teaspoon mustard powder
1 teaspoon wine vinegar
1 teaspoon lemon juice
4 teaspoons oil
⅓ teaspoon Madras curry powder
⅓ teaspoon turmeric
freshly milled black pepper
1 dessertspoon mayonnaise

For the garnish: 1 teaspoon fresh chopped parsley

First hardboil the egg by placing it in cold water, bringing it up to the boil and boiling for 7 minutes. Then cool it under cold running water.

While the egg is boiling, cook the pasta: bring a small saucepan of water up to boiling point with some salt and a few drops of oil in it, then add the pasta, stir a couple of times and let it simmer for 10 minutes. Then tip it into a colander (or sieve) and run the cold tap on it to cool it (or it will become sticky).

Leave it to drain now and meanwhile make up the dressing by combining all the ingredients except for the mayonnaise. Next, place the macaroni, pepper, onion and apple in a salad bowl, peel and chop the hardboiled egg quite small, and add that too. Now stir in the mayonnaise and mix well, followed by the dressing. Have another good mix to get all the ingredients coated with the dressing, then serve the salad on crisp lettuce leaves, sprinkled with parsley.

Left: Michael's mango fool, page 206; Rhubarb and orange shortcake crumble, page 211.

Egg and anchovy salad with herbs

Sliced runner beans could be used for this instead of string beans. And if no fresh herbs are available, use the finely chopped green part of the spring onion with some parsley.

2 large eggs
6–8 oz new potatoes (175–225 g), washed not scraped
2 oz green string beans (50 g), topped and tailed
3 spring onions, chopped finely
crisp lettuce leaves
1 small tin anchovy fillets, well drained
a few black olives or capers
1 tablespoon fresh chopped herbs (chives, tarragon, parsley, etc)

For the dressing:

½ level teaspoon mustard powder
1 small clove of garlic, crushed
1 teaspoon wine vinegar
3 tablespoons olive oil
salt and freshly milled black pepper

Begin by making up the dressing by combining all the ingredients in a screwtop jar and shaking vigorously to blend everything evenly. Then cook the new potatoes, which will only need about 15 minutes or so, depending on size. About five minutes before you think they're done, add the beans to the saucepan and let them cook on top of the potatoes in the steam for 5 minutes.

Then drain them both in a colander and when they're cool enough to handle slice the potatoes, and snip the beans into 1 inch (2·5 cm) lengths. Place them together in a serving bowl and toss them around in half the salad dressing while they're still warm.

Next place the eggs in cold water in a small saucepan, bring them up to the boil and when they've reached that point boil them for 7 minutes. After that cool them under a cold running tap until they're quite cold. Now peel the eggs and chop them roughly, then add them to the potatoes and beans together with the spring onions, and mix well with the rest of the dressing.

Now on a serving plate arrange the lettuce leaves as a base, then pile the salad mixture on top, garnish it with the anchovy fillets arranged in a criss-cross pattern, and finally sprinkle over the olives and herbs.

Serve the salad with crusty French bread, and a glass of chilled Provençale Rosé would be just the right accompaniment.

Brown rice and raw vegetable salad

You can use a combination of any raw vegetables for this (grated parsnip, celeriac, for instance), or indeed whatever salad vegetables you happen to have available. However, this is how I make it.

brown rice measured to the 2 fl oz level in a glass measuring jug (60 ml)
1 tablespoon finely chopped Chinese leaves or any cabbage
1 dessertspoon coarsely grated carrot
1 dessertspoon finely chopped dessert apple
1 dessertspoon finely chopped celery
1 tablespoon chopped watercress
2 spring onions, finely chopped
1 dessertspoon walnuts, chopped
1 quantity of vinaigrette dressing (*see page 171*)

Cook the rice as described on *page 134*, then tip it into a serving bowl, and while it's still warm pour on half the dressing. Fork it lightly to distribute the dressing but don't do any hefty stirring or the rice grains will break and the whole thing will go stodgy.

Now leave the rice to cool, then mix in the chopped Chinese leaves, carrot, apple, celery, watercress and half the spring onion. Then pour on the rest of the dressing, mix lightly again, then sprinkle on the walnuts and the rest of the spring onion as a garnish.

Marinated kipper and potato salad

If you have time to organise the kippers the night before you need them, I would recommend it as their taste improves the longer they are in the marinade. In summer it is best made with new potatoes, but in winter a firm red Desirée potato would do well.

6–8 oz potatoes (175–225 g)
4 oz kipper fillets (110 g)
1 small onion, chopped small
1 bayleaf
1 dessertspoon fresh chopped parsley

For the dressing:

1½ fl oz olive oil (40 ml)
1 tablespoon red wine vinegar
1 level teaspoon soft brown sugar
1 dessertspoon lemon juice
1 level teaspoon mustard powder
½ teaspoon dried dill
a dash of Tabasco

Begin by placing the kipper fillets, folded, in a jug and pouring boiling water over them. Then place a plate on top of the jug and leave them for 6 minutes.

Meanwhile make up the dressing by placing all the ingredients in a screwtop jar, putting the lid on firmly and shaking vigorously to get everything blended well. Now drain the kippers and dry them with kitchen paper.

Next slice each fillet diagonally into strips about ½ inch (1 cm) wide and place these in a shallow dish along with the bayleaf, chopped onion and the dressing. Mix them well but carefully, to avoid breaking up the kipper pieces, then cover with clingfilm and leave in the fridge until you're ready for them – but at any rate for a minimum of an hour.

To serve, boil the potatoes till tender, then drain them and chop into ½ inch (1 cm) cubes. Place them in a serving dish and pour the kipper and all the dressing over the potatoes while they're still warm. Mix again thoroughly, sprinkle on the chopped parsley, then you can either eat it straightaway or else wait until the potatoes have cooled.

Marinated prawn salad

This won't take any more than 10 minutes of your time, then while it marinates you can go off and have a bath, read the paper or mow the lawn knowing that a delicious supper awaits you. Even better, invest 10 minutes the night before, as a longer marinating period will be an improvement.

4 oz peeled prawns (110 g), defrost if frozen

For the marinade:

2 tablespoons olive oil

juice of half a lemon

⅛ teaspoon dried dill

½ teaspoon fresh ginger, grated

2 small spring onions, finely chopped

salt and freshly milled black pepper

To serve:

1 tablespoon mayonnaise

few drops of Tabasco

4 pitted black olives, cut into quarters

2 firm tomatoes, skinned, deseeded and chopped

1 small spring onion, finely chopped

crisp lettuce leaves

Place the prawns in a small saucepan with 2 tablespoons of olive oil, the juice of half a lemon, the dill and the grated ginger, and season with salt and pepper. Now bring the whole lot slowly up to simmering point, simmer for one minute then remove from the heat.

Add the chopped spring onions to the prawns then pour it all into a jug so that the prawns are completely covered with the marinade. Leave them (covered) in the fridge for at least an hour, or better still overnight.

When you're ready to serve them, tip them into a sieve placed over a bowl and drain off all the marinade and discard it. Now in a bowl mix the prawns with a level tablespoon of mayonnaise and a few drops of Tabasco. Serve the prawns on a bed of crisp lettuce leaves and garnish with the chopped olives and tomatoes, and with the spring onion sprinkled over.

This could be served with a small rice salad to make it more substantial – though I must say I prefer it just on the lettuce and with lots of crusty bread.

Fennel salad à la Grecque

In the summer this makes a wonderful partner to some cold poached fish or cold chicken. (Actually I like it just as it is, with lots of crusty bread to mop up the juices!)

½ **fennel bulb, trimmed** (*see page 181*)
8 oz tomatoes (225 g), skinned and chopped, or a small tin of Italian tomatoes, chopped
12 black peppercorns, coarsely crushed
⅓ **teaspoon coriander seeds**
1 tablespoon olive oil
1 small onion, chopped
1 small clove of garlic, crushed
1 dessertspoon wine vinegar
1 dessertspoon lemon juice
⅓ **teaspoon oregano**
1 teaspoon tomato purée mixed with 4 fl oz water (110 ml)
2 spring onions, finely chopped
1 teaspoon fresh chopped parsley
salt

First cut the half-bulb of fennel in half lengthways, trim away a little of the central stalk at the base, then cut the two pieces lengthways again and separate out the layers.

Now crush the peppercorns and coriander seeds, using a pestle and mortar or else the end of a rolling-pin and a basin. Next heat the oil in a medium-sized saucepan and fry the onion gently for 5 minutes, then add the crushed peppercorns, coriander and garlic and continue to cook gently for a further 5 minutes. After that add the wine vinegar, lemon juice, chopped tomatoes, oregano and the tomato purée-and-water.

Add the fennel to the saucepan, pushing it down into the liquid and add a little salt, then, keeping the heat low, let it simmer gently for 20 minutes (stirring it once or twice during that time) or until it is tender yet retains some bite. Then transfer it, with the juices, to a shallow serving dish to cool. When it's quite cold, sprinkle with the spring onion and parsley.

Lentil and mushroom salad with green peppercorns

This is part of a Mixed Double – with vegetarian moussaka (page 149) or sautéed spiced vegetables with lentils (page 152). If you cook 2 oz (50 g) of lentils instead of just the 1 oz (25 g) needed for this recipe, you can reserve the rest for the moussaka and save yourself some time. The green (unripened) peppercorns come preserved in brine in small jars and give just the right boost in flavour to this recipe – so do the similar pink peppercorns, if you want to vary it slightly.

1 oz cooked whole lentils (25 g) (gently simmered for 30 minutes in 2 fl oz, 55 ml, water)
1½ oz small pink-gilled mushrooms (40 g), thinly sliced
2 spring onions, finely chopped
1 rounded teaspoon green peppercorns

For the dressing:
½ clove of garlic
½ teaspoon rock salt
½ teaspoon mustard powder
1 tablespoon lemon juice
2 tablespoons olive oil

This couldn't be easier. All you do is combine the raw mushrooms, cooked lentils and chopped spring onions with the green peppercorns in a salad bowl. Then crush the garlic together with the salt with a pestle and mortar until you get a smooth paste, then add the mustard powder, followed by the lemon juice and finally the oil. Whisk the dressing to get everything evenly combined, then pour it over the salad. Toss the ingredients together, and leave for a good half an hour before serving.

Tuna and pasta salad with tarragon and lemon dressing

If you want a light meal in a hurry, then this will take you barely fifteen minutes from start to finish. If you're extra hungry, I suggest you use 2 oz (50 g) of pasta.

3¾ oz tin of tuna fish (100 g)
1½ oz wholewheat macaroni (40 g)
½ medium onion, thinly sliced and separated out into rings
1 rounded tablespoon fresh chopped parsley

For the dressing:

½ teaspoon tarragon, fresh or dried
1 dessertspoon lemon juice
½ teaspoon grated lemon zest
1 small clove of garlic
½ level teaspoon salt
½ level teaspoon mustard powder
2 dessertspoons olive oil
1 dessertspoon tuna oil (from the tin)
freshly milled black pepper

To serve: a few crisp lettuce leaves

First cook the macaroni in plenty of salted boiling water to which a few drops of oil have been added (if it is wholewheat it will need 10 minutes after coming to the boil, otherwise 8 minutes). After that, drain it in a colander, then sluice it under a cold running tap to cool it quickly – or else it will go sticky.

While the pasta's cooking, you can make up the dressing. Using a pestle and mortar, pound the garlic, tarragon and salt to a paste and after that add the mustard powder and some freshly milled pepper, followed by the lemon juice. Mix again quite thoroughly, then add the olive oil and tuna oil (which can be drained into a spoon straight from the tin). Lastly add the lemon zest and give everything another good mix.

Now flake the tuna fish into a salad bowl. Then place a double sheet of absorbent kitchen paper on a flat surface and tip the cooled pasta onto it. Dry it a bit to get rid of any excess moisture before adding it to the tuna. Then add the onion rings to the salad, and pour the dressing all over. Toss all the ingredients well together, and serve the salad on a bed of lettuce leaves with the parsley sprinkled over.

Chinese beansprout and watercress salad

This is a salad with a delightfully fresh, crunchy texture and a soy sauce dressing that's full of flavour.

2 oz fresh beansprouts (50 g)
1 oz sliced raw mushrooms (25 g)
2 spring onions, finely chopped
2 inches of cucumber (5 cm), chopped small
approx 1 tablespoon watercress leaves

For the dressing:

1 dessertspoon soy sauce
1 dessertspoon wine vinegar
2 dessertspoons oil
1 rounded teaspoon tomato purée
½ teaspoon mustard powder
½ teaspoon freshly grated root ginger
½ clove of garlic, crushed
freshly milled black pepper

This is utterly simple. All you do is assemble all the salad ingredients together in a serving bowl and mix them around a bit. Then measure all the dressing ingredients into a bowl and whisk them together – or else place them in a screwtop jar and shake briskly to amalgamate them well. Then toss the salad thoroughly in the dressing – and that's it.

Chicken Waldorf salad

This would make a perfect main-course salad for a hot summer's day, served on a bed of crisp lettuce and garnished with watercress. A Marks & Spencer cooked chicken leg portion is the perfect size.

1 cooked chicken joint (approx 7 oz, 200 g)
1 stick of celery (1 oz, 25 g), chopped
2 spring onions, chopped, including some of the green part
½ oz walnuts (10 g), roughly chopped
8 black grapes, halved and depipped

For the dressing:

½ teaspoon tarragon, fresh or dried
⅓ teaspoon rock salt
½ clove of garlic
1 rounded tablespoon mayonnaise
1 heaped dessertspoon natural yoghurt
freshly milled black pepper

For the garnish: lettuce leaves and watercress

Begin by stripping the skin from the chicken and discarding it. Then remove the flesh from the bones and slice it into longish, 1 inch (2·5 cm) thick pieces, and place these in a bowl. Then add the chopped celery to the bowl, together with the spring onion and chopped walnuts.

Now for the dressing: if you are using fresh tarragon, chop it and add it to the chicken. If dried, then put half a teaspoonful into a mortar along with ⅓ teaspoon of rock salt and half a clove of garlic: then pound these to a paste. After that add the mayonnaise and yoghurt with a few twists of freshly milled pepper, then blend everything together thoroughly.

Pour the dressing over the salad and toss everything together well to get a good coating of the dressing. Arrange some lettuce leaves in a shallow serving dish, pile the chicken salad on top, sprinkle the grapes all over, and garnish with sprigs of watercress.

Vinaigrette

These are the basic quanti-ties needed to make sufficient vinaigrette to dress an ordinary green or mixed salad for one. Note: they do not necessarily correspond with similar dress-ings in recipes in this chapter – because certain kinds of salad may need more or less dressing.

1 small clove of garlic
⅓ teaspoon rock salt
½ teaspoon mustard powder
freshly milled black pepper
1½ teaspoons wine vinegar
3 dessertspoons olive oil

Using a pestle and mortar (or failing that, a basin and the end of a rolling-pin) crush the clove of garlic together with the salt, mustard powder and a couple of twists of freshly milled pepper until you have a thick paste.

Then add the wine vinegar and whisk with a fork to amalgamate the paste with the vinegar. Finally pour in the olive oil and continue to whisk vigorously with a fork to blend everything together thoroughly. Store the vinaigrette in a screwtop jar – not for more than a few hours – and shake the jar well to recombine all the ingredients before pouring over the salad.

Note: this quantity would be ideal for serving with half an avocado served on a bed of crisp lettuce leaves and a few sprigs of watercress or another interesting way to serve half an avocado is to peel it and slice it and serve it with sliced firm tomatoes with the dressing spooned over for an *avocado and tomato salad.*

Mayonnaise

Is it really worthwhile for one person to make their own home-made mayonnaise, you're probably asking already. My answer is that it is by using the following quick method, because it is infinitely better than the commercial variety, even the better brands. Using the blender method below it is no trouble at all to make; you can make ¼ pint (150 ml) in one go (in fact it's difficult to make less!), and then store in a screwtop jar in the refrigerator for up to a fortnight to use as and when you need it. It can also form the basis of other sauces, such as tartare sauce (see below).

Quick mayonnaise

This is mayonnaise made in a blender or food processor, and takes only two minutes. Because you're using a whole egg (rather than just the yolk) the problem of curdling is eliminated. The finished product is not as 'wobbly' as authentic mayonnaise, but it is very good.

1 large egg
¼ pint groundnut oil (150 ml)
½ teaspoon mustard powder
freshly milled black pepper
½ teaspoon salt
drop of white wine vinegar

Break the egg straight into the goblet of your blender or food processor, then sprinkle the mustard powder, pepper and salt on top of it. Have the groundnut oil measured out ready in a glass measuring jug, then switch the machine on. Now pour the oil – in a thin and steady trickle – through the hole in the top onto the rotating blades. When all the oil is in, switch the machine off and add literally a drop of wine vinegar and blend this in. Spoon the mayonnaise into a screwtop jar, seal well and store in the fridge until required (up to a fortnight).

Note: for a *garlic mayonnaise* add 1 crushed clove of garlic to this mixture, but only just before you intend to use it (i.e. don't store the mayonnaise with the garlic in it).

Tartare sauce

This, too, is infinitely preferable to the shop-bought varieties. It will store for up to two weeks in the fridge well sealed in a screwtop jar. Use it in recipes (for example in plaice fillets tartare, see page 78) or just as an accompaniment to plain grilled or fried fish.

1 quantity of quick mayonnaise (as above)
4 teaspoons capers, drained
4 small gherkins
1 clove of garlic, crushed
1 level teaspoon chopped parsley or fresh tarragon
salt and freshly milled black pepper

Quite simply, chop the drained capers roughly and slice the gherkins lengthways and then across as finely as possible. Stir these into the mayonnaise, together with the garlic, parsley, and some seasoning. Mix well till thoroughly blended, then store in a screwtop jar in the fridge.

Vegetable Variations

One is fun!

Fresh vegetables are a must for anyone wanting an interesting and varied diet: simply following their seasonal changes provides a stimulating choice all the year round (with prices, of course, that are at their cheapest). I have constantly made the point that imported new potatoes in February, for example, are tasteless and a waste of money – as would be imported new carrots in May. There's something aesthetically appealing to me about a selection of fresh, brightly coloured vegetables in their season – the complete antithesis of the depressing sight of a freezerful of uniform plastic bags sitting uninvitingly in the foggy mist. Having said all that, I would qualify it just by saying that I am not against all imports: some, like mange-tout, haricot vert, aubergines, peppers and courgettes, help immensely to put a little life into the leaner winter months.

Purists would have us shopping for our vegetables fresh each day, but life is just not like that. Single people have problems with shopping and storing that families do not have, and compromise is inevitable. I have written at some length about this problem at the beginning of this book (*see page 12*), so all I will add here is to say that as many nutrients are lost by careless preparation and cooking of vegetables as are ever forfeited by having to store them. Which may explain why in this chapter you will find very little reference to boiling, and quite a lot to stir-frying.

Quick stir-fried red cabbage

Although spiced red cabbage slowly baked in the oven in the Eastern European way is a firm favourite of mine, I also like it cooked quickly on top of the stove as in this recipe. It can transform even the plainest sausage, gammon steak or pork chop into something quite special.

4–5 oz red cabbage (110–150 g)
1 very small or half a medium Cox's apple
½ small onion, chopped
½ oz butter (10 g)
1 teaspoon oil
1 clove of garlic, chopped
⅛ teaspoon powdered cloves
⅛ teaspoon powdered cinnamon
a few gratings of whole nutmeg
½ teaspoon brown sugar
1 dessertspoon wine vinegar
salt and freshly milled black pepper

You need to shred the cabbage quite finely into ¼ inch (5 mm) shreds, discarding any tough stalky bits. Chop the apple quite small but leave the skin on (it improves the flavour).

Now in a large, heavy-based frying-pan melt the butter and oil, then stir in the onion and cook it for 2–3 minutes before adding the apple and garlic. Continue to cook for 2–3 minutes, then turn the heat up to high, add the cabbage and stir-fry it by keeping it on the move with a wooden spoon, so that it all comes into contact with the heat at the base of the pan. After five minutes or so it should have shrunk a bit, so at this point sprinkle in the spices and a seasoning of salt and pepper, then turn the heat down and let it go on cooking for a further 10 minutes, stirring it once or twice during that time. Bite a piece to see if it's tender and when it's ready turn the heat up again, sprinkle in the sugar and vinegar. Stir everything thoroughly, then serve.

Cheese and onion rosti

This is a variation on the traditional Swiss method of cooking potato. The result is a much more substantial accompaniment to cold meats, sausages, plain chops or steaks.

½ lb potatoes (225 g), approximately two medium-sized potatoes
2 rashers of bacon, chopped very small
½ medium onion, grated
1 oz grated cheese (25 g) – you could use a Swiss cheese such as Emmenthal or, just as good, a strong Cheddar
2 tablespoons of oil
salt and freshly milled black pepper

First of all peel the potatoes, then cover them with boiling water and boil them for just 10 minutes, so that they are still firm. Then drain them and either leave them to cool or (if you're in a hurry) run them under cold water to get them cool enough to handle.

While that's happening, cook the little pieces of bacon in a little oil until they are crisp and golden-brown (it will only take a minute or so). When the potatoes have cooled grate them, using the coarse side of the grater, straight into a large mixing bowl. Then gently (so as not to break up the potato) stir in the grated onion and cheese, followed by the bacon and a good seasoning of salt and pepper.

Next heat two tablespoons of oil in a frying-pan to very hot, then transfer the potato mixture to the pan and, using a spatula and/or a wooden spoon, pat the mixture (again, gently) into a flattened disc-shape.

Keep the heat fairly low and cook for 7–10 minutes, then when the underside is golden-brown, turn the rosti over (with the aid of a slice or spatula) and cook for the same length of time on the other side. Serve straightaway.

Note: you must have the oil very hot for this or the rosti might stick (it also needs a good solid-based frying-pan or non-stick pan).

Mushrooms in garlic butter

This recipe, I have to confess at once, is strictly for garlic lovers.

4 oz mushrooms (110 g), sliced
1 oz butter (25 g)
1 fat clove of garlic, finely chopped
1 teaspoon lemon juice
1 teaspoon fresh chopped parsley
salt and freshly milled black pepper

In a medium-sized saucepan melt the butter, and when it begins to foam add the mushrooms and garlic and stir them around to get a good coating of butter. (It will look as if you have far too much in the pan, but fear not, it will shrink a lot.) Season with salt, pepper and lemon juice. Then keeping the heat low cover the pan with a lid and let the warmth draw out their juices for 5 minutes. After that remove the lid and go on stewing them gently for 10–15 minutes or until all the juices have evaporated. Serve sprinkled with the chopped parsley.

Leek fritters

Although it's true these delicious little fritters do need to be deep-fried, it's still a quick recipe. All the preparation can be done while the oil's heating and after that they take barely a minute to cook. Many other vegetables can be cooked in this way, courgettes cut into chip-shapes or slices of aubergine or onion rings.

2 medium leeks, trimmed and washed

2 tablespoons flour, seasoned with a little salt

1 egg white

oil for deep-frying

First fill a saucepan (that will take a small deep-frying basket) with oil up to one-third full, then start to heat it up.

To prepare the leeks, slice the white parts across into ¼ inch (5 mm) thick rings. Then sift the seasoned flour onto a flat plate and coat the slices of leek on both sides with the flour. Now with an electric hand-whisk, beat up the egg white until it has reached the soft-peak stage (i.e. it stands up in little peaks when you lift the whisk out of it), then check to see the oil has reached the required temperature. If you have a cooking thermometer the right temperature is 360°F (185°C). If not, pop a cube of bread into the oil and if it turns golden-brown in one minute, it's ready. Now dip each of the floured leek slices in the beaten egg white and place in a deep-frying basket. Lower it gently into the oil and cook until the coating has turned golden-brown all over – don't go away because this will only take a minute or so. Drain the fritters on crumpled greaseproof paper or kitchen paper and serve straightaway sprinkled with crushed rock salt and freshly milled black pepper.

Potatoes Niçoise

These are so delightful I could eat a plateful of them on their own! Otherwise they will partner almost anything from fried eggs to fillet steak.

5 oz potatoes (150 g), weighed after peeling
¼ green pepper or red, finely chopped
1 small onion, finely chopped
1 clove of garlic, finely chopped
2 ripe red tomatoes, skinned and chopped, or 2 dessertspoons of tinned Italian chopped tomatoes
1 teaspoon fresh chopped herbs or parsley (fresh rosemary leaves, bruised and then finely chopped, would be good)
2 black olives, chopped
1 tablespoon olive oil
salt and freshly milled black pepper

For this you need to chop the potatoes into ¼ inch (5 mm) cubes then dry them very thoroughly with kitchen paper or a clean tea-cloth. Now heat the oil in a heavy-based 7 inch (18 cm) frying-pan and when it's very hot, add the potato cubes along with the chopped pepper. Fry these over a medium heat for 5 minutes before adding the onion and the chopped garlic, then continue to cook for a further 5–10 minutes or until the vegetables are tender and a nice crusted golden colour.

At this stage add the tomatoes and herbs and turn the heat up. Cook for a further 2 minutes (or until the tomatoes have dried off and nicely coated the potatoes). Season the potatoes with salt and pepper and sprinkle with the chopped olives.

Note: some chopped bacon fried with the onion is a nice addition. You can also make a beautiful flat omelette out of this with two beaten eggs poured in and finished off under the grill.

Sautéed fennel with Parmesan

Fennel is a rather neglected vegetable in this country: its texture is similar to celery but it has a delicate aniseed flavour. When you buy one, I suggest you use half of it for this recipe (which is sufficient as an accompanying vegetable), and use the other half later for fennel salad à la Grecque (see page 166).

½ bulb of fennel (see below)
1 teaspoon butter
1 teaspoon oil
1 tablespoon grated Parmesan cheese
salt and freshly milled black pepper

To prepare the fennel bulb, trim off the green shoot by cutting diagonally to make a V-shape, then slice off the root part at the other end, and remove any tough or brown outer layers. Now slice the bulb in half widthways: you can now wrap one half in clingfilm to store in the refrigerator for use at a later time.

Cut the other half into two quarters, take a little of the stalky core out but not all of it because you want the layers, including the green centre part, to stay intact. Place the quarters in a small saucepan, cover them with boiling water, add a little salt, then simmer for about 10 minutes or until they feel tender when tested with a skewer.

Now drain them in a colander (by the way, if you want to reserve the water, it makes a good stock for soups). Next melt the butter with the oil in the same pan, and when it is hot add the drained fennel and cook until tinged with gold on all sides. While it's still in the saucepan, sprinkle each piece with half the Parmesan, allow it to melt a little over the heat, then serve with a seasoning of salt and pepper and the rest of the Parmesan sprinkled over.

Note: if you are lucky enough to buy a fennel bulb with the green leafy fronds, these can be chopped like parsley and sprinkled over at the end like a garnish.

Stir-fried mange-tout

A packet of these little green flat pea-pods usually weighs 6 oz (175 g), so you can cook half in the conventional way for one meal (with a knob of butter, salt and pepper in a small covered saucepan: on a low heat they will cook in their own juices in 6–10 minutes). The rest can be used later in the week with the following recipe.

---

3 oz mange-tout (75 g), topped and tailed

½ teaspoon grated fresh root ginger

½ teaspoon soy sauce

---

1 dessertspoon dry sherry

---

1 dessertspoon water

---

1 dessertspoon oil

Put the oil and ginger in a 7 inch (18 cm) frying-pan together, then slowly heat the oil with the heat turned to low for about 10 minutes so that the fresh ginger flavour really permeates the oil. Then turn the heat up high and add the mange-tout, stirring them and moving them constantly around in the hot oil until they are paler in colour and begin to cook (about 1 minute).

Then mix the sherry, soy sauce and water together, and pour the mixture over the mange-tout, still stirring everything around. Next put a lid on the pan and let them cook for about 5 minutes, being careful though not to overcook them – they do need to be quite crunchy. These go well with any of the pork dishes.

Note: for a change you could cut these into ½ inch (1 cm) diagonal slices.

Chinese stir-fried green vegetables

Don't worry if you can only buy large amounts of these vegetables: all of them will keep for up to five days protected in a polythene bag in the refrigerator. So you don't have to use them all at once. Because I rather like mixing eastern and western foods, I have to say that this little lot goes beautifully with bangers and mash!

2 oz broccoli (calabrese) (50 g)
2 oz Chinese leaves or other cabbage (50 g)
1 medium leek
1 spring onion, finely chopped
1 tablespoon groundnut oil
1 level teaspoon freshly grated ginger
1 small clove of garlic, sliced
1 tablespoon dry sherry *mixed with* 1 teaspoon soy sauce and 1 tablespoon of water

Note: no salt is added to this (until it reaches the table) because the soy sauce is already quite salty.

For *stir-fried cabbage* you may use the above method with 6 oz (175 g) of any shredded green cabbage and it will take 2 minutes' initial frying time and 4–6 minutes after the liquid has been added.

For this recipe you will need a large, heavy-based frying-pan. Anyway, first prepare the vegetables, starting with the broccoli. Snip off the flowery heads and separate them into smallish pieces, while the stalk bits should be sliced diagonally quite thinly. Slice the Chinese leaves across into 1 inch (2·5 cm) rounds, then slice these dividing them in two.

Slice the leek vertically almost through, then fan it out under a cold running tap to remove any grit from between the layers. Then dry it and slice it completely in half lengthways then cut it across into 1 inch (2·5 cm) rounds (which will then separate out into little squares).

When you're ready to cook the vegetables, heat the oil to very hot then add the ginger and cook that for about 30 seconds, stirring it around all the time. Next add the garlic, followed by the broccoli – stir it around and keep it on the move for about 1 minute, then add the Chinese leaves and leek. Keep stirring everything around the pan for another minute, making sure everything makes contact with the very hot base of the pan.

Now add the spring onions and then the sherry-and-soy mixture, and let the whole lot go on cooking for a further 4–5 minutes (depending on how crisp you like your vegetables). Then serve straightaway.

Chinese stir-fried beansprouts

This is a fresh-tasting, crisp vegetable dish that can be served with almost anything.

4–6 oz fresh beansprouts (110–175 g)
1 oz carrot (25 g) – that is half a small carrot
1 oz celery (25 g)
2 small or 1 large spring onion
1 dessertspoon oil
½ clove of garlic, crushed
½ teaspoon grated fresh root ginger
1 dessertspoon soy sauce
1 tablespoon dry sherry

Begin by preparing the vegetables: cut the carrot into slices lengthways, then cut these slices into matchstick-sized strips. Do the same with the celery. The spring onions should be halved lengthways (using most of the green part as well), then each half cut in half again and the layers separated out into small thin strips.

Now, in a heavy-based 7 inch (18 cm) frying-pan, heat the oil with the heat turned high, and when it's hot add the garlic, ginger, carrot and celery. Then stir these around the pan while they're cooking for 30 seconds, and after that add the beansprouts and spring onions. Now stir everything around constantly so that all the pieces of vegetable come into contact with the heat, then after 1 minute pour in the sherry and soy sauce. Continue to stir the vegetables for 1 minute more, then serve straightaway.

Note: if you bought an 8 oz (225 g) packet of beansprouts, how about using the rest for the salad on *page 169*?

Quick braised celery with carrots and onions

One of the beauties of this recipe is that you can use parts of the celery you might otherwise be tempted to throw away. If you're using the slightly tough outer stalks, just pare off the stringy bits with a sharp knife.

1 large stick of celery
2 oz carrot (50 g)
½ oz butter (10 g)
1 small onion, chopped
¼ teaspoon celery seeds, if available
2 fl oz water (55 ml)
fresh chopped parsley
salt and freshly milled black pepper

Trim the celery stalk, cut it in half lengthways, then cut these lengths into 2 inch (5 cm) pieces. The carrot should be cut into strips the size of very small chips.

Now in a small saucepan melt the butter, stir in the onion and cook it for a minute or so before adding the carrot and then the celery. Toss everything around in the hot fat until they get nicely tinged golden at the edges – this will take about 3–4 minutes.

Next sprinkle in the celery seeds, then pour in the water, add some salt and pepper, cover with a tight-fitting lid, turn the heat down and simmer for about 5 minutes or until tender. After that, uncover the pan, turn the heat up and boil briskly until the liquid has reduced to about a tablespoon (approximately 5 minutes). Then serve the celery and carrot, with the juice, and some parsley sprinkled over.

Jacket potatoes with leeks, bacon and cheese

If you're not in a hurry, a jacket potato with an interesting stuffing makes a self-contained supper dish for one. If you feel guilty about heating the oven up just for this, then put another one in to cook at the same time and use it the next day for salmon and caper fish cakes (see page 73).

1 large (7 oz, 200 g) potato
olive oil
½ oz butter (10 g)
1 tablespoon cream or top of the milk
1 leek, washed and chopped fairly small (about 3 oz, 75 g)
3 rashers of smoked back bacon, chopped
1½ oz grated Cheddar cheese (40 g)

Preheat the oven to gas mark 6, 400°F, 200°C

Scrub the potato clean first of all and dry it thoroughly with a clean tea-cloth, then smear the surface of the skin with olive oil. Now thread the potato onto a long skewer (this helps to conduct the heat to the centre of the potato while it's cooking). Sprinkle the skin with a little salt, then put it on the highest shelf in the oven and bake for one hour – turning the potato over at half-time.

Towards the end of the cooking time heat the butter in a frying-pan and fry the chopped bacon until it's fairly crisp, then remove it to a plate to keep warm. Now add the leek to the pan and stir it around to cook and soften for 5–6 minutes. Then preheat the grill.

When the potato is ready, remove it from the skewer and cut it in half. Now using a spoon scrape out all the potato flesh from inside the skin into a bowl; add the butter, cream, bacon and leek (plus all the buttery pan juices) and mix everything evenly together. Season with salt and pepper, then spoon the mixture back into the potato shells and place them on a gratin dish. Sprinkle the tops of both halves with the cheese then place under the grill until the cheese is brown and bubbling.

Jacket potatoes with cottage cheese and chives

This variation is more suitable for a vegetarian. You prepare and bake the jacket potato as in the above recipe, but use the following filling.

1 heaped tablespoon cottage cheese
1 tablespoon natural yoghurt
1 dessertspoon snipped chives or very finely chopped spring onion
salt and freshly milled black pepper

For the topping:

1½ oz grated Cheddar cheese (40 g)
1 spring onion, finely chopped
1 clove of garlic, finely chopped
1 dessertspoon breadcrumbs

As in the preceding recipe scoop out the cooked potato into a bowl, then thoroughly mix it with the cottage cheese, yoghurt, chives and a seasoning of salt and pepper. Then spoon it back into the potato shells.

Mix the topping ingredients together, then sprinkle over the potato halves. Place the halves on a gratin dish and grill until the tops are browned and bubbling. Serve with a crisp green salad.

Super Snacks

Achoïade

Mozzarella in carrozza

Devilled mushrooms

Individual Alpine egg

Cheese and chutney puff

Stilton and celery savoury

Pan-fried pizza

Pizza Amalfitan

Pizza with salami and mushrooms

Crumpet pizza

Kipper pâté

One is fun!

I'm not absolutely sure how to define a snack, but for me it is a light something that provides a quick lunch or supper dish rather than the main meal of the day. The following recipes have been selected on that premise, and I have tried to take into account the impromptu nature of making a snack so that the main ingredients are store-cupboard standbys and things readily to hand.

One of the handy things about snack cookery (for want of a better word) is that it lends itself to imaginative ways of using up, well, not leftovers, but all sorts of things that linger on unused. Hardened ends of cheeses that have lurked ignored at the back of the fridge become transformed when grated and melted under the grill. Likewise anything toasted takes care of stale bread – especially French bread, which never keeps fresh longer than a day. If you cut it into diagonal slices and toast them, you can then top them with the Stilton and celery savoury (which also helps to account for the odd egg that has passed its poaching peak) or with anchoïade, perhaps the nicest of all snacks.

So don't despair that you didn't have time to get to the shops today. Settle down in front of a good TV programme with a super snack and a glass of wine, and still feel cosseted!

Anchoïade

This is a really gutsy snack, served on toasted French bread, and redolent of sunny picnics in Provence! If you're wondering what to do with the rest of the anchovy fillets, cover them in a bowl with clingfilm and store to use later for the crumpet and individual pizzas (see pages 197–8) – another Mixed Double.

6 anchovy fillets, drained
1 clove of garlic, crushed
6 black olives, stoned and finely chopped
½ small onion, finely chopped
1 ripe tomato, skinned and chopped, or use 1 tablespoon tinned chopped Italian tomatoes
1 heaped dessertspoon fresh chopped parsley
½ teaspoon dried oregano
1 heaped teaspoon tomato purée
couple of drops of wine vinegar
oil
freshly milled black pepper

Serve with: a 4–5 inch (10–13 cm) slice from a French loaf

Start off by pounding the anchovy fillets to a pulp, either by using a pestle and mortar or else by putting them in a basin and crushing them with the end of a rolling-pin. Then spoon them out into a bowl, and add the garlic, chopped olives and onion, and the tomato and parsley. Now sprinkle in the oregano and a seasoning of pepper, and add the tomato purée, vinegar and a few drops of oil. Use a fork to mash everything together until thoroughly combined.

Next heat up the grill, and slice the French bread in half horizontally. Place both pieces under the grill, crust-side up, to crisp them up a little (but not brown them). Then spread half of the anchoïade mixture on each of the slices – on the untoasted side – bringing the topping right up to the edges of the bread. Put them back under the grill with a little drizzling of oil on each piece, to heat through for 5 minutes. Then serve.

Mozzarella in carrozza

Literally 'Mozzarella in a carriage' – the carriage being two slices of bread dipped in beaten egg and deep-fried. It makes a delicious, quick snack. I've found the addition of a slice of ham (better still, Parma ham) provides an interesting variation.

2 slices of white bread from a large loaf or its equivalent
1¼ oz Mozzarella cheese (30 g), sliced thinly
1 egg
1 tablespoon milk
1 dessertspoon seasoned flour
oil for frying

Prepare the 'carriage' simply by placing the slices of Mozzarella between two slices of bread (unbuttered). Next beat up the egg together with the milk and pour it into a shallow dish (to make coating easier). Spread the seasoned flour out on a largish plate – and now you're ready to go.

Pour about 1 inch (2·5 cm) of oil into a wide saucepan, or even a frying-pan, and heat it up to 360°F (185°C) or to the point where a cube of bread thrown in turns golden-brown in one minute. Then coat both sides of the sandwich with seasoned flour, and then cut the sandwich into four quarters. Dip each quarter into the beaten egg and milk to soak up the mixture on both sides. Now place the quarters in a deep-frying basket or else lower them into the hot oil with the aid of a fish slice.

They will probably float on top of the oil to a certain extent, so cook them for 30 seconds on one side, then use the slice to turn them over to cook for a further 30 seconds on the other side. When the coating is a nice golden-brown, they're ready. Drain them on crumpled greaseproof paper, then serve.

Devilled mushrooms

These can be served on toasted bread or French bread, or with triangles of bread fried in bacon fat. Alternatively they make a good topping for a pan-fried pizza (see page 196).

6 oz mushrooms (175 g)
½ medium onion, chopped
1 oz butter (25 g)
½ teaspoon mustard powder
3 tablespoons red wine
1 tablespoon red wine vinegar
a few drops of Worcestershire sauce
a few drops of Tabasco sauce
1 dessertspoon plain flour
salt and cayenne pepper

Start off by heating up the butter in a medium-sized frying-pan then soften the onion in it for about 5 minutes – without letting it brown. Now wipe – but don't peel – the mushrooms and slice them fairly thinly. Add them to the pan and let them cook gently for 5 minutes.

Meanwhile, in a basin, combine the mustard powder with the wine and wine vinegar, and sprinkle in a few drops of Worcestershire sauce and a dash of Tabasco (if you like your mushrooms very devilled, you can add two dashes, but don't overdo it).

Next sprinkle the flour over the onion and mushrooms and stir it in to absorb the juices, then leave to cook very gently for a couple of minutes before pouring in the wine-and-vinegar mixture. Give it all a good stir, then cover the pan with a lid or plate and leave to simmer gently for 10 minutes. Then remove the lid, season with salt and a little cayenne, and if there is quite a lot of liquid left, cook briskly until it has reduced to a sauce-like consistency.

Individual Alpine egg

This is an old favourite of mine: blissfully simple but perfect for a quick snack served with wholewheat 'soldiers'. If you want to make it more substantial, double the ingredients and use a 4 inch (10 cm) ramekin.

1 large egg
2 oz grated cheese (any kind of hard cheese) (50 g)
salt and freshly milled black pepper

Preheat the oven to gas mark 4, 350°F, 180°C. You'll need a 3½ inch (8 cm) diameter ramekin.

All you do, in fact, is put half the grated cheese into the ramekin (no need to butter it), then carefully break the egg on top of the cheese, and finally sprinkle the rest of the cheese over.

Place the dish on a high shelf in the oven and bake it for 15 minutes, by which time it will have puffed up, almost like a soufflé, and the cheese will be bubbling, and the egg just set.

Cheese and chutney puff

This is a very superior version of toasted cheese: the chutney gives it a distinctive flavour, and the egg gives it lightness.

3 oz strong Cheddar cheese (75 g)
1 dessertspoon chutney or Branston pickle
2 slices of bread
1 small egg, beaten
butter
salt and freshly milled black pepper

Note: instead of the chutney, you could use raw grated onion or crisp crumbled bacon.

Preheat the grill, and while it's warming up grate the cheese into a bowl and stir the chutney (or pickle) into it. Next toast the slices of bread under the grill on one side only, then lightly butter the untoasted side.

Now lay a sheet of foil over the grill rack and arrange the toast slices on it (buttered-side up). Then beat the egg in a separate bowl and pour it into the cheese-and-chutney mixture. Season with salt and pepper, and mix well with a fork until thoroughly blended.

Pile the cheese-and-egg mixture on the toasted slices and place them under the grill – not too near (approximately 4 inches, 10 cm). Grill until the cheese has puffed up nicely and turned golden-brown on top – about five minutes.

Stilton and celery savoury

This is a wonderful recipe for using up odd bits of Stilton that never got eaten. Excellent served with grilled, or fried, tomatoes and lots of watercress.

1½ oz Stilton cheese (40 g), grated
½ oz butter (10 g)
½ oz flour (10 g)
½ teaspoon mustard
2 fl oz milk (55 ml)
1 egg yolk
½ stick of celery, very finely chopped
1 spring onion, finely chopped, or ¼ onion, grated
cayenne pepper
salt and freshly milled black pepper

Serve with: 2 thick slices of toasted bread, buttered

First preheat the grill, then in a small saucepan melt the butter and stir in the flour and mustard. Keep stirring till smooth then gradually add the milk, bit by bit, still stirring until you have a smooth glossy paste. Now remove the pan from the heat and beat in the egg yolk, followed by the cheese, celery and onion. Season with salt and freshly milled black pepper.

At this stage you can see to the toast – butter it quite generously, then spread the cheese mixture all over both slices, taking it right up to the edges. Sprinkle each one with a pinch of cayenne, then place them under the grill for about 3–5 minutes or until the cheese is browned and bubbling.

Pan-fried pizza

A pizza makes a perfect snack meal for one and this particular recipe (the basis of which I learned from Elizabeth David in her lovely book Italian Food) *is made very quickly indeed in a frying-pan. The toppings, of course, are flexible: once you have made this a few times and got the feel of it, you can be wonderfully inventive.*

4 oz plain flour (110 g)
1 teaspoon baking powder
½ teaspoon salt
freshly milled black pepper
½ teaspoon oregano
approx 3 tablespoons water mixed with 1 tablespoon of oil
additional oil for frying

Start off by measuring the flour and baking powder, salt, pepper and oregano in a mixing bowl and mix them together. Then, in a cup, combine the oil and water and pour this into the dry mixture. Now using a wooden spoon, stir to form a moist but unsticky dough, then transfer this to a floured working surface and knead it a little before rolling – or patting – out to a 7 inch (18 cm) diameter round.

Now heat up a solid-based 7 inch (18 cm) frying-pan before adding sufficient oil to give you a depth of about ¼ inch (½ cm). When the oil is hot slip in the round of dough and cook over a moderate heat for 5 minutes. While it's cooking liberally oil a dinner plate, and as soon as the base of the pizza is nicely browned invert it onto the oiled plate, then slip the dough straight back into the pan to cook the other side until nicely browned. Your pizza base is now ready for the topping of your choice.

Pizza Amalfitan

Here is one suggestion for a topping for your pizza base, a particularly colourful one!

1 pizza base (as above)
4 tomatoes, thinly sliced
½ a 6 oz (175 g) Mozzarella, diced
½ teaspoon dried basil
4–6 anchovy fillets, drained and split in half lengthways
2 teaspoons drained capers
6 black olives, stoned and sliced
a little oil
salt and freshly milled black pepper

When the pizza base is cooked on both sides, preheat the grill. Now arrange the sliced tomatoes over the pizza base, then sprinkle with the diced Mozzarella and basil. Arrange the sliced anchovy fillets in a criss-cross pattern over next, then sprinkle on the capers and olives.

Drizzle a little oil over the top of the pizza, season with freshly milled pepper but not too much salt (because of the saltiness of the anchovies) then transfer to cook under the grill for 5 minutes until the top is browned and bubbling. Then eat it straightaway.

Pizza with salami and mushrooms

One more idea for a topping. For this you can use any snack salami sausage (there's one widely available now called Peperami) or Italian pepperoni-type sausage.

3 oz mushrooms (75 g), sliced if large
a few sprigs of parsley
2 spring onions, trimmed
1 clove of garlic
2 tablespoons tomato purée
1 salami snack sausage
1 tablespoon grated Parmesan
a little oil

When the pizza dough is ready, preheat the grill. Now pile the mushrooms, parsley, spring onions and garlic onto a chopping board and chop them all finely. (Alternatively you can whizz them all together in a food processor, until they are finely but not minutely chopped.)

Next spread the tomato purée all over the pizza base, then top with the mushroom-and-onion mixture. Slice the salami sausage thinly and diagonally and scatter the pieces over the top of the pizza. Finally season with salt and pepper then sprinkle with the Parmesan. Drizzle a little oil over the surface of the pizza and transfer to cook under the grill for 4–5 minutes. Then serve immediately.

Crumpet pizzas

These are undoubtedly a snack – they will take just ten minutes to make from start to finish – but they are still reasonably substantial, and they fill the kitchen with a distinctly pizzeria *aroma!*

---

3 crumpets

butter

1½ oz strong Cheddar cheese (40 g)

1 small tomato, sliced

3 anchovy fillets, drained

3 black olives, stoned and halved

¾ teaspoon mixed herbs

olive oil

salt and freshly milled black pepper

First preheat the grill to high, then toast the crumpets very lightly and butter them quite generously. Next cut the cheese into thinnish slices and arrange them so that they cover the surface of each crumpet. Then pop a slice of tomato (or one and a half slices) on top of the cheese.

Slice each anchovy fillet in half lengthways and arrange the two halves in a cross over the cheese and tomatoes. Place a half olive in two of the segments on each crumpet, sprinkle the mixed herbs over and a seasoning of salt and pepper, then drizzle a minute quantity of olive oil over the top of each pizza. Pop them all under the grill until everything is sizzling and bubbling – about 4–5 minutes. And if you serve with a glass of something Italian, you'll enjoy a fair reward for very little effort.

Kipper pâté

You could use frozen kipper fillets for this, but even better would be a proper kipper. By the time you've removed the skin and bones from one medium-sized kipper you should be left with approximately 4 oz (110 g) of fish.

4 oz kipper (110 g)
1½ oz softened butter (40 g)
2 large or 4 small spring onions, finely chopped
1 dessertspoon fresh chopped parsley
2 teaspoons lemon juice
a little freshly grated nutmeg
salt and freshly milled black pepper

To serve: lemon wedge
cayenne pepper

First of all cook the kipper by removing the heads, folding the sides of the fish together and packing it vertically in a tall warmed jug. Then pour in enough boiling water to cover the kipper, put a plate on top of the jug and leave in a warm place for 6 minutes. (If using frozen fillets, cook according to the instructions on the packet.) When the fish is cool remove all the skin and bones, and flake the flesh into a bowl.

Now, using a fork, mash vigorously until you have a paste. Then add the butter, bit by bit, continuing to mash until it is all thoroughly incorporated. Next add the chopped spring onion and parsley, the lemon juice and a good grating of nutmeg. Season with salt and pepper (being a bit sparing with the salt) then give the pâté a final mashing till evenly blended.

Pack the mixture into a 4 inch (10 cm) ramekin, cover with clingfilm, then chill in the fridge for at least 2 or 3 hours. Serve with a lemon wedge, a dusting of cayenne and some hot buttered toast.

Happy Endings

Poached pear with caramel sauce

Butterscotch bananas

Individual crème caramel

Michael's mango fool

Individual bread-and-butter pudding

Chocolate mocha mousse

Jamaican bananas

Raspberry shortcake crumble

Prune and apricot compote

Orange and apricot soufflé omelette

Muesli biscuits

One is fun!

The question I get asked more often than almost any other is 'how do you manage not to put on weight in your job?' The stock answer is that I eat very little sugar; indeed I've discovered over the years that the less sugar you eat, the less you want. Sugar is addictive and unfortunately many of us are made addicts at a very early age. But it *is* a habit that can be shaken off gradually – until in the end it can be difficult to cope with over-sweetness (for instance I am now unable to eat muesli or other breakfast cereals that are ready sweetened). Sugar is also a superfluous food if we are eating a balanced diet, so for reasons of health (not to mention vanity) it's the number one food to cut down on if there's a weight problem.

At this point I hasten to add that I don't believe in the total abandonment of sugar, and I still greatly enjoy something sweet and fattening once a week. Sunday in our household is the feast day, and on that day I have no compunction at all in indulging in a cake or pudding or bar of chocolate (or all three).

So this is a chapter for *your* feast days. For rounding off your meal on other days I recommend a selection of fresh fruits, and to make it more interesting, how about some of the more exotic fruits that are now becoming more widely available?

Cape gooseberry: remove the papery husks, then eat whole.
Fresh fig: eat peeled or not, according to taste.
Guava: cut in half and scoop the flesh from the skin.
Kiwifruit: peel, then cut into slices or wedges.
Lychee: remove brittle shell and central stone.
Mango: cut a thick slice vertically from top of fruit as near to the stone as possible, then repeat the cut on the other side. Then scoop out the flesh from the two shells.
Passion Fruit: cut in half and scoop out juicy seeds with a spoon.
Paw Paw: prepare in the same way as melons.
Persimmon (Sharon Fruit): slice off the top and scoop out the pulp.
Ugli Fruit: prepare and eat in the same way as orange or grapefruit.

Poached pear with caramel sauce

This makes just the right-sized, and most attractive, sweet for one. This idea also works very well with a poached peach (see below).

1 medium-sized pear
1¼ pints water (720 ml)
1 oz sugar (25 g)
1 vanilla pod

For the sauce:

1 oz light soft brown sugar (25 g)
1 tablespoon tap-hot water
2½ fl oz single cream (60 ml)

Begin by peeling the pear, trying to keep its shape and leaving the stalk intact (apart from looking nice, it will help you to handle the pear when it's cooked). Then cut a thin slice from the base of the pear so that it will be able to stand up in the serving bowl.

Pour the water into a small saucepan and add the sugar. Start to bring it up to simmering point, and when the sugar has dissolved add the pear and vanilla pod. Once the water has started to simmer, give the pear 10–15 minutes' poaching (this will depend entirely on how hard it is). Turn it over in the water during the cooking and test it for tenderness with a skewer.

Meanwhile make the caramel sauce by placing the light brown sugar in a small pan and melting it over a medium heat. Cook it until it has turned a gingery colour, then take it off the heat and add 1 tablespoon of tap-hot water: it will sizzle and splutter a bit but will soon subside. Cook it gently for another 30 seconds, then leave it to cool slightly – for a minute or so – then stir in the cream until smooth.

Now drain the pear, using the stalk to lift it out of the pan. Let it cool then sit it upright in a glass serving dish. Spoon the caramel sauce over it, then chill in the fridge till needed.

Note: in the summer, this works extremely well with a peach. To poach it, follow the same method as for the pear but when the sugar has dissolved place the peach, whole and unpeeled, in the water. Cover with a lid and poach for 10 minutes, then drain it and slip the skin off before setting it in a serving bowl.

Butter-scotch bananas

This is a lovely sticky sauce – just made for bananas, especially if you serve it hot, poured over bananas and ice-cream.

1 banana
1 portion of vanilla ice-cream

For the butterscotch sauce:

½ oz butter (10 g)
1 oz soft brown sugar (25 g)
1 tablespoon golden syrup
1 tablespoon cream

Place the butter, sugar and syrup in a thick-based saucepan, then over a very low heat simply allow the ingredients slowly to dissolve and liquefy – this can take about 10–15 minutes. Then stir to make sure all the sugar is dissolved and, when it is, turn off the heat and add the cream.

Then arrange the ice-cream and sliced banana in a serving dish, and pour the hot sauce over. A few chopped nuts would be a nice addition.

Individual crème caramel

This is a one-person portion (a man-sized portion almost!) that is made in a 4½ inch (11 cm) ramekin. It is possible, I've discovered, to cook it on top of the stove (see below) but I have to say I've come to the conclusion it's less bother in the oven.

2½ fl oz double cream (60 ml)
1½ fl oz milk (40 ml)
1 egg
1 dessertspoon soft brown sugar
1 oz granulated sugar (25 g)
a drop of vanilla essence
1 tablespoon warm water

Preheat the oven to gas mark 2, 300°F, 150°C

Start off by placing the granulated sugar in a small pan and put it on a medium heat to start melting. It will soon begin to turn brown and then darken. Give it a stir to help dissolve all the granules and when it has started bubbling and has turned a couple of shades darker than golden syrup, take it off the heat and carefully add the tablespoon of warm water. It will splutter but soon subside. Stir, and when the syrup is smooth again quickly pour it into the ramekin.

Now pour the cream and milk into another small pan and leave it to heat while you whisk the egg together with the brown sugar and a drop of vanilla essence in a bowl. When the cream and milk is hot, pour it onto the egg mixture and whisk again thoroughly. Then pour this into the ramekin on top of the caramel.

Place the ramekin in a roasting tin, pour an inch or two of boiling water into the tin, then transfer the tin to the centre of the oven and bake for 30–35 minutes. After that leave the crème caramel to cool, then chill it in the fridge. To serve, loosen the edge with a palette knife and invert it onto a serving plate.

Note: to cook it on top of the stove, you need to have a saucepan that will take the ramekin with room enough for you to lift it in and out. When the mixture is ready to be cooked, place the ramekin on a saucer (or milk saver) in the saucepan then carefully pour in boiling water to come no more than three-quarters of the way up the ramekin. Simmer gently making sure it does not simmer too fast, and place a plate or saucer over the top of the ramekin to prevent any water getting in. Simmer for 50 minutes or so, then preheat the grill and finish off by placing the ramekin under the hot grill (approx 4 inches (10 cm) from the heat) to cook the top for 10 minutes.

Michael's mango fool

I happen to love the taste of fresh mangoes on their own (a combination of peaches and cream all in one fruit, I think). But as my husband rightly points out, you very often find the mango has ripened beyond the point where it can be decently served as a fruit. So, on those occasions, this is what he does with them.

1 ripe mango
2 fl oz double cream (55 ml)
1 teaspoon caster sugar

Slice the mango in half lengthways around the stone and pull the two halves apart. With mangoes the flesh does tend to cling hard to the stone, but the beauty of this recipe is that it doesn't matter. Pull the two halves apart then, using a teaspoon, scrape all the orange flesh out of the two shells into a nylon sieve. Then scrape off any flesh left clinging to the stone, too.

Set the sieve over a bowl then take a wooden spoon and press all the fruit through the sieve until all the purée is in the bowl and only any fibrous bits left in the sieve. Then, using an electric whisk, whip the cream until thickened. Stir the sugar into the mango purée then, with a metal spoon, fold the purée into the cream. Pour the whole lot into a stemmed glass, cover the glass with clingfilm then leave the fool to chill in the fridge for at least a couple of hours.

Individual bread-and-butter pudding

The traditional recipe for this age-old favourite can be adapted for one person. With the quantities below it works best in a 4 inch (10 cm) diameter ramekin dish.

2 slices of bread from a small loaf
a little butter
1 teaspoon candied lemon or orange peel
¾ oz currants (20 g)
2½ fl oz milk (60 ml)
2 tablespoons double cream
¾ oz caster sugar (20 g)
¼ teaspoon grated lemon rind
1 small egg
freshly grated nutmeg

Preheat the oven to gas mark 4, 350°F, 180°C

First butter the inside of the ramekin, smearing the butter on with kitchen paper. Then slice the bread – not too thickly – and butter the slices, leaving the crusts on. Now you will have to trim the slices of bread to fit into the ramekin, so do this with half of it to make one layer of buttered bread over the base of the dish.

Sprinkle the candied peel and half the currants over this layer, then trim the rest of the bread to form another layer on top. Sprinkle the rest of the currants on top. Next, in a glass measuring jug, measure out the milk and stir in the cream, followed by the sugar and lemon rind. Now whisk the egg, first on its own and then into the milk mixture. Pour the whole lot over the bread, then sprinkle over some freshly grated nutmeg.

Bake in the oven for 35 minutes, until the top is golden-brown. In this size dish the pudding will rise up almost alarmingly, but don't worry, as it cools it will settle back into the dish.

Chocolate mocha mousse

I think if you're going to make a mousse for yourself then you deserve to get plenty of flavour from it – and this one certainly offers that!

2 oz plain chocolate (50 g)
1 egg, separated
1 dessertspoon rum
1 slightly rounded teaspoon coffee granules

To serve:

1 fl oz pouring cream (25 ml)
1 level teaspoon coffee granules, dissolved in 1 teaspoon warm water
grated chocolate

Start off by setting a small basin over a small pan of barely simmering water, then add the coffee granules to the basin. Measure in 2 teaspoons of hot water and stir to dissolve the granules. Now break up the chocolate into small pieces, add these to the basin and stir till the chocolate has melted and been incorporated with the coffee and you have smooth sauce.

Next separate the egg, the white into a medium-sized bowl and the yolk into a smaller one. Beat up the yolk then stir it well into the chocolate mixture, off the heat. Now stir the rum into it, and leave to cool for about 10 minutes.

Meanwhile whisk up the egg white to the soft-peak stage (that is, when it leaves soft peaks when you lift the whisk out of it). Then, using a metal spoon fold the egg white into the chocolate mixture. Spoon the whole lot into a stemmed wine glass, cover with clingfilm and chill for a couple of hours. To serve: combine the cream with the dissolved coffee, pour this over the top of the mousse and sprinkle with a little grated chocolate.

Jamaican bananas

The delightful thing about bananas is that they seem to have been created ready-packaged for one. This recipe is rather special if you include the rum; if you replace it with lemon juice that would be very good, too.

1 banana
½ oz raisins (10 g)
1 dessertspoon rum
1 dessertspoon orange juice
½ teaspoon grated orange zest
1 tablespoon dark soft brown sugar

You'll also need a gratin dish

Start off about half an hour before you cook the banana by placing the raisins in a small basin and sprinkling the rum (or lemon juice) over them. Then leave them to soak for about 30 minutes.

When you're ready, preheat the grill, then butter a gratin dish. Sprinkle half the sugar over the base. Next peel the banana and split it in half lengthways and lay it (round-side uppermost) on the sugar. Sprinkle the rum and raisins over the fruit, followed by the orange zest. Pour in the orange juice and, finally, sprinkle over the remaining sugar.

Now cover the dish with foil and place it under the grill at a distance of 4 inches (10 cm) from the heat and cook for about 15 minutes. Then remove the foil, give it a couple of minutes more under the grill, then serve immediately.

Raspberry shortcake crumble

This is what I suppose I should call a 'master recipe' as it can be varied in endless ways. Some of these alternatives I've outlined below, but raspberries are perhaps the nicest filling (and the frozen variety makes it possible to use them all year round).

3 oz fresh or frozen raspberries (75 g)

1 level dessertspoon caster or granulated sugar

For the topping:

1½ oz self-raising white or wholewheat flour (40 g)

¾ oz butter or margarine (20 g)

1 oz light soft brown sugar (25 g)

Preheat the oven to gas mark 4, 350°F, 180°C. You'll also need a 4 inch (10 cm) ramekin, well buttered.

Simply place all the topping ingredients in a mixing bowl and rub them lightly together, using your fingertips, until you have a uniform mixture that resembles fine breadcrumbs.

Next arrange the raspberries in the ramekin and sprinkle them with the sugar. Now top the raspberries with the crumble mixture, pressing it down lightly to get it even all over, then run a fork gently over the surface to make it crumbly. Bake it on the high shelf in the oven for 20–25 minutes or until the top is golden. Serve it warm with chilled pouring cream.

Note: an alternative topping for this could be 2 oz (50 g) wholewheat flour, 1 oz (25 g) demerara sugar, 1 oz (25 g) butter and 1 heaped teaspoon of chopped, toasted hazelnuts. This topping would also be suitable for the fillings opposite.

Rhubarb and orange filling

This is probably nicest of all in February when the first silken pink rhubarb stalks appear.

4 oz rhubarb (110 g), cut into 1 inch (2·5 cm) chunks
grated zest of half a small orange
1 heaped tablespoon sugar

Place the rhubarb in a small saucepan together with the sugar and orange zest, then set it over a gentle heat for 5 minutes or just until the juice begins to run (you don't need to cook it). Now pile everything into a 4 inch (10 cm) ramekin, sprinkle the crumble mixture over the surface as above, and bake for 20–25 minutes.

For *rhubarb and ginger filling*: instead of the orange zest, use a small piece of preserved ginger finely chopped.

Gooseberry filling

4 oz gooseberries (110 g), topped and tailed
1 rounded tablespoon sugar

Treat the gooseberries in exactly the same way as the rhubarb above.

Dried apricot and almond filling

For this you place 3 oz (75 g) of dried apricots in a small saucepan (no need to presoak them), then add the juice of a small orange, 1 dessert-spoon of brown sugar and enough cold water to just cover the fruit.

Then simmer gently for 10–15 minutes. Meanwhile cut three whole blanched almonds into slices lengthways. Then pile the apricots (plus any juice) with the almond slices into a 4 inch (10 cm) ramekin, top with the crumble mixture and bake as above.

Note: an alternative topping for this might be 1½ oz (40 g) wholewheat flour, ½ oz (10 g) ground almonds, 1 oz (25 g) demerara sugar and 1 oz (25 g) butter.

Prune and apricot compote

1 oz prunes (25 g)
1 oz raisins (25 g)
2 oz dried apricots (50 g)
1 rounded dessertspoon demerara sugar
zest and juice of half an orange
5 fl oz water (150 ml)

To serve:

2 tablespoons natural yoghurt
½ oz chopped toasted hazelnuts (10 g)

Dried fruits make a lovely salad, and the bonus is that what you don't need for this recipe will keep quite happily in the storecupboard.

You need to start this off the night before by placing the prunes, raisins and apricots in a small bowl and covering them with the water (make sure all the fruit is immersed) then leave them to soak overnight.

The next day transfer the fruit and their soaking water to a small pan, then add the sugar. Cover the pan and bring to simmering point, then leave to simmer gently for about 10 minutes or until all the fruit feels tender when tested with a skewer. Next stir in the orange zest and juice, then tip the whole lot into a shallow serving bowl to cool and when cold, cover with clingfilm and chill in the fridge.

Just before serving, spoon the yoghurt on top and sprinkle the toasted hazelnuts on top of that.

Orange and apricot soufflé omelette

If you feel like something sweet, light and made in moments – this is it. You can use other varieties of jam (strawberry, for instance, or even marmalade) to vary it slightly. It's probably very fattening, so don't have it too often!

2 eggs
1 oz caster sugar (25 g)
grated rind of a quarter of an orange
½ oz butter (10 g)
1 rounded tablespoon apricot jam, warmed slightly
1 teaspoon orange juice

First separate the eggs and place the whites in a clean, grease-free bowl. Then in another bowl add the sugar to the yolks and beat until thick, pale and lemon-coloured, then stir in the orange rind. Next whisk the egg whites until just stiff and fold them into the egg-yolk mixture carefully, using a metal spoon. At this stage, preheat the grill.

Now heat the butter in a 7 inch (18 cm) frying-pan until foaming and pour in the mixture. Cook over a fairly low heat until the underside of the omelette is golden (don't attempt to stir the mixture – in fact, don't touch it at all except to find out how the underside is cooking by lifting with a palette knife).

Transfer the pan to sit under the grill and cook for about 2 minutes or until the omelette has puffed up and the surface is golden-brown. While that's happening, mix the orange juice with the warmed jam in a cup or jug, then when the omelette is ready pour this mixture over one half and fold the other half over. Sprinkle the surface with a little sugar and serve straight onto a warmed plate – not worrying too much if the folding-over bit isn't too neat.

Muesli biscuits

If you're wondering if it is worth making homemade biscuits for one, I am offering you this recipe to prove that it is. They are extremely quick and *easy to make, and store well in an airtight tin so that you've always got something to munch with your cup of tea.*

5 oz unsweetened muesli (150 g), available from wholefood stores

3 oz butter or margarine (75 g)

3 oz demerara sugar (75 g)

Preheat the oven to gas mark 5, 375°F, 190°C

Start off by melting the butter gently in a saucepan – don't let it colour. Meanwhile mix the demerara sugar and the muesli together in a mixing bowl. Then pour the melted butter into the muesli mixture and mix everything together so that it's thoroughly blended.

Now butter a shallow baking tin (measuring 11 × 7 inches, 28 × 18 cm), and press the biscuit mixture all over the base of the tin, making sure it goes right up to the edges and into the corners. Level off the top with the back of a tablespoon, then bake in the centre of the oven for 15 minutes or until it has turned a pale golden colour.

Remove the tin from the oven and cut the mixture into 12 portions while it's still warm. Then leave it in the tin until quite cold and crisp. Use a palette knife to lift the individual biscuits out, then store in an airtight tin.

Useful Addresses

All the addresses below have a mail-order service if you ring and check for current prices.

General kitchen equipment

Elizabeth David Ltd.,
46 Bourne Street,
London SW1W 8JB

(01-730 3123)

David Mellor,
4 Sloane Square,
London SW1W 8EE

(01-730 4259)

Divertimenti Co Ltd.,
68-72 Marylebone Lane,
London W1M 5SF

(01-935 0689)

Kitchen knives and small implements

Lesway (Victorinox Distributors),
3 Clarendon Terrace,
Maida Vale,
London W9 1BZ

(01-289 7197)

Specialised Chinese foods

Cheong Leen Supermarket,
4-10 Tower Street,
London WC2H 9NR

(01-836 5378)

Specialised Indian foods

A and N Sharma,
241 Camden High Street,
London NW1

(01-485 2533)

Index

Italic entries refer to illustrations.

N

O

P

One is fun!